# Programming Games for Intellivision

Óscar Toledo Gutiérrez

**Programming Games for Intellivision**

Copyright © 2018 Óscar Toledo Gutiérrez

ISBN: 978-1-387-92908-5

Official website: **http://nanochess.org/**

The author welcomes your comments, suggestions and errata reports, please send them to: **biyubi@gmail.com**

You can also follow him on Twitter as **@nanochess**

First published in 2018

*Dedicated to my beloved wife Rosa Nely and our little fairies Myriam Sofia and Samantha.*

*For Adan and Cecilia, now both can read my book.*

*For Elisa, keep smiling.*

*For my mother and my father, thanks for all the advice.*

# Contents

## The Book

**Foreword**
Dawn of a revolution.................................................................v

**Preface**
What am I trying to do here? ...................................................vii

**Acknowledgments**
For all the good people ..............................................................ix

**Chapter 1**
Intellivision architecture............................................................1

    1.1 Architecture ..................................................................1

    1.2 Flash cartridges ...........................................................2

    1.3 IntyBASIC ...................................................................4

**Chapter 2**
IntyBASIC setup ........................................................................5

**Chapter 3**
Programming with IntyBASIC ....................................................9

    3.1 Our first IntyBASIC program .....................................12

    3.2 Our first SPRITE...........................................................15

3.3 Controlling the game ........................................................16

3.4 Add a title screen ............................................................18

3.5 Sound ...............................................................................19

## Chapter 4
A Game of Ball ......................................................................27

4.1 Setting up the graphics ...................................................27

4.2 Drawing the playfield .....................................................29

4.3 Paddles .............................................................................31

4.4 The ball .............................................................................32

4.5 Sound ...............................................................................37

## Chapter 5
Monkey Moon ........................................................................39

5.1 Planning ...........................................................................39

5.2 Code for graphics ............................................................40

5.3 The level ...........................................................................44

5.4 The player .........................................................................47

5.5 Ladders .............................................................................51

5.6 This game can be won ......................................................53

5.7 Throw some lunar rocks ...................................................55

5.8 Player dies ........................................................................58

5.9 Jumping ............................................................................60

5.10 Sound and final details ...................................................62

## Chapter 6
Space Raider ...........................................................................65

6.1 A stars background ...........................................................69

6.2 A player and his bullet.................................................71

6.3 Enemies everywhere .....................................................73

6.4 Battle in space ...............................................................77

6.5 More attack waves.........................................................80

6.6 The title screen .............................................................85

## Chapter 7
Bouncy Cube...........................................................................89

7.1 Displaying the title screen............................................93

7.2 The player......................................................................95

7.3 The level......................................................................102

7.4 Scrolling the level .......................................................108

7.5 The player....................................................................109

7.6 Explosion.....................................................................114

7.7 Sound effects ..............................................................116

7.8 Music ..........................................................................117

## Chapter 8
Assembly language ...............................................................121

## Appendix A
IntyBASIC Reference Manual ...............................................131

A.1 IntyBASIC language specification................................134

A.2 Expression syntax  .....................................................160

A.3 Assembly language interfacing ..................................170

A.4 Some further notes .....................................................171

A.5 Real number of variables allowed..............................174

A.6 Generating ROM for Nostalgia emulator....................174

A.7 Source code debugging ................................................175

**Appendix B**
AY-3-8914 reference ..........................................................177

**Appendix C**
Useful resources................................................................181

**Appendix D**
Source code for rotating smiley ...........................................183

**Appendix E**
About the author ...............................................................187

# Foreword

## Dawn of a revolution

At the dawn of the video game revolution, almost all video games were dedicated units. The concept of a 'program cartridge' was foreign to many people until systems such as the Atari VCS and Mattel Intellivision gained prominence in the late 1970s.

The games for these popular video game systems were usually written using computers that cost well beyond what any video game fan was capable of purchasing. Doing any sort of programming was impossible for the vast majority of people until computers such as the Vic 20 and Atari 400/800 began to be sold in stores. Would-be Intellivision programmers were thwarted by the lack of a means of talking to the device.

Finally, in the late 1990s, enough information was available in order to create a development system. At long last, Intellivision fans had the capability to finally start developing new games for their favorite system!

However, the excitement was short lived for most, as they soon discovered that programming the system was not as simple as they once hoped. The new development kit required the programmer to write programs in CP1610 assembly code. Still, determined programmers came out with some very impressive new games. Unfortunately, the capability to write new games was still far beyond the casual fan. That is, until Óscar Toledo Gutiérrez decided to write IntyBASIC for the system! The ability to simplify the game making process has allowed Intellivision fans from around the world to fulfill their dream of creating something for the system.

As a publisher, I was skeptical as to the ability of IntyBASIC to create a game that I would wish to publish. I was wrong. A couple of Elektronite games have been already written in IntyBASIC and are a couple of the best!

Thanks to Intellivision Basic, now you too can fulfill your desire to create the next Intellivision game masterpiece!

This book tells you how. Enjoy!

*William M. Moeller*
*President of Classic Game Publishers, Inc.*
*Elektronite*

# Preface

## What am I trying to do here?

I was invited to give a presentation at a conference at a local university in Mexico, and I could pick any technical subject I wanted. I decided to speak about writing an Intellivision game in one hour.

Why one hour? It's the time that it took me to write a game after I completed the first working version of the IntyBASIC compiler.

What's IntyBASIC? It's an integer-based language compiler based on the old and popular BASIC language, with extensions for Intellivision hardware. With it, you can write a complete game without even resorting to assembler language.

Even better, if you have the algorithm of a game in your head (or on paper) you can quickly code an Intellivision version of the same game because BASIC is almost like English.

But of course, first you must learn IntyBASIC and so here is the book.

I intend to start from simple things and progress step by step to bigger things, or in other words, start with small example programs and then progress to medium games and then to bigger games.

When I was young I learned programming by entering BASIC games published in books and magazines. I believe typing these programs in key by key was fundamental, because someday you're going to type your own programs.

I learned a lot, and even more from the games published over several issues, because while another issue came out I would stare at the screen trying to understand what's going on with the current section of code.

So for the four main games in this book, I present each one in sections, adding code blocks each time, so you can understand the development process in a simple way.

I strongly suggest to type in the games manually instead of downloading everything from http://nanochess.org/games_book.html and going straight to playing the games.

I hope you'll enjoy the ride!

*Óscar Toledo G.*
*July 2018*

# Acknowledgments

## For all the good people

IntyBASIC would have never flown so high without the help of the following members of Atariage that contributed valuable advice, test programs and even support libraries: ARTRAG, atari2600land, awhite2600, carlsson, catsfolly, ckblackm, CrazyBoss, Cybearg, DZ-Jay, First Spear, freewheel, GroovyBee, intvnut, Jess Ragan, Kiwi, mmarrero, RevEng, SpiceWare and Tarzilla.

Many thanks to Joe Zbiciak for creating the jzintv emulator and its utilities like the as1600 assembler, a software foundation used heavily by IntyBASIC.

Special thanks to Albert Yarusso, founder of AtariAge for his kindness hosting the IntyBASIC forums and contests.

Thanks to Jason Schelhorn (gemintronic) and Anders Carlsson (carlsson) for their suggestions reading the book and testing the examples provided.

William M. Moeller revised the historical facts provided in chapter 1 and proofread it. Chris Derrig (Kiwi) and Luc Miron (Pixelboy) proofread the entire book. Joe Zbiciak (intvnut) revised the technical facts and provided a friendly description of the sound mixer in Appendix B.

I owe these people a great debt of gratitude because a man is nothing without friends.

Thanks to all!

# Chapter 1

## Intellivision architecture

The Intellivision console was Mattel's answer to the wildly successful Atari VCS (Video Computer System), which was released in 1977.

The Mattel Intellivision was developed in 1978, test-marketed in 1979 and then widely released in the USA in 1980.

Like the Atari console, the Intellivision uses cartridges for its games. However, unlike the Atari's simple joystick and button, the Intellivision controller has a 16 direction disc, keypad buttons from 0-9, Clear and Enter keys, plus 4 side buttons.

### 1.1 Architecture

The Intellivision disc is like a joystick, but only requires a finger (or thumb) to select one of its 16 directions. Most game systems of the era used only 8 directions.

The Intellivision display is 159x96 pixels with 16 colors, arranged in a 20x12 grid which can display letters, numbers and graphics. The system also has support for 8 moveable objects (or 'sprites') over the screen. The Intellivision is easier to program than the Atari VCS but the system display is not as flexible and prevents users from implementing display tricks that are possible on the Atari machine.

The Graphic ROM or 'GROM' contains 256 predefined 8x8 pixel graphics called 'cards'. The Graphic RAM or 'GRAM' allows the user to define up to 64 'cards' of the same size. A complete Intellivision screen has 240 cards. This means that the user cannot fill an entire screen with user defined graphics. However, some tricks can be used in order to make it happen.

The system's sound generation is handed by the General Instruments AY-3-8914 sound chip, which is very similar to the AY-3-8910 sound chip used in many arcade games, consoles such as Vectrex, and computers such as the Spectrum 128, Amstrad, the British ORIC-1 and the Japanese MSX computers.

The AY-3-8914 is capable of handling 3 tone channels with 16 levels of volume and a noise generator. The same chip has inputs for reading the controllers and keypads.

The Central Processor Unit (CPU) used in the Intellivision is the General Instruments CP1610. This 16-bit processor is able to address 64K words, with each word being 16 bits. (128K bytes was amazing for the time.)

When the Intellivision master component was developed, memory was very expensive. As a result, the system contains only 240 bytes of 8-bit memory and 352 words of 16-bit memory (240 being used for the 20x12 card screen array). Also, there are 512 bytes of definable graphics RAM that are only accessible during the vertical blanking period.

## 1.2 Flash cartridges

After its commercial demise in 1991, the Intellivision was largely forgotten until Carl Mueller Jr. began to create the world's first Intellivision emulator on the PC. William Moeller and Scott Nudds gave Carl technical support by dumping the Graphics ROM, Executive ROM, ECS Executive ROM and all of the system's game ROMs. Technical information on the system was compiled.

Eventually, this effort was purchased by Intellivision Productions, Inc. and released as the Intellivision Lives! CD.

These emulation efforts led to the revealing of enough technical information that eventually Joe Zbiciak was able to create a publicly available development kit and create his own emulator which is still supported to this day!

The first 'homebrew' games were eventually developed thanks to the combined efforts of many people who are too numerous to mention.

Flash cartridges, such as the Intellicart, the Cuttle Cart 3 and more recently, LTO Flash! were developed for the system. These cartridges allow game ROMs to be loaded and played on the system. Furthermore, it also allows programmers willing to explore the depths of the Intellivision to create their own games!

Despite these tools being available to adventurous programmers, all new games were required to be programmed in CP1610 assembly code.

Assembly code allows the programmer to use the maximum speed of the console. The Intellivision runs at 3.579545 mhz divided by 4, which is approximately 895 khz (PAL models are slightly faster at 1 mhz).

Each instruction takes 8 to 9 cycles to execute on average, this means the Intellivision can process around 102000 instructions per second, which is much slower than the Z80 processors used in consoles such as the Colecovision, which is able to process 716000 simple instructions per second.

The advantage of the Intellivision processor is it ability to process 16-bit wide data in a single instruction. An 8-bit processor like the Z80 would require several instructions to accomplish the same thing! The CP1610 also includes several advanced instructions, like bit shifting for 1 or 2 bits.

Being forced to use assembler code, programming the Intellivision is a very time consuming endeavor. Despite the efforts required, some very impressive new games have been developed, such as Space Patrol, D2K Arcade and Christmas Carol vs The Ghost of Christmas Presents.

## 1.3 IntyBASIC

The IntyBASIC compiler was a project that I started to ease the development time for new games and to simplify Intellivision programming efforts.

The first version labeled '0.1' was posted on January 27th, 2014 on the Atariage Intellivision programming forum (a required visit for any Intellivision developer)

It follows the conventions of "standard" BASIC, but without line numbers similar to MS-QBasic included with MS-DOS 5.

The easiness of programming with IntyBASIC allowed the number of games being developed for Intellivision to increase rapidly.

For example, you can compile these two lines:

```
PRINT AT 0 COLOR 7,"Hello world"
WHILE 1: WEND
```

And after passing through IntyBASIC and the assembler as1600 it generates a program that works right away. You can load it directly into your emulator or Flash cartridge without further effort.

Before IntyBASIC, it took at least 50 lines of code to create something similar, requiring knowledge about the cartridge header, the address for assembling, the characters codes, the location of the screen in memory and writing routines for clearing the screen and copying data into the screen.

Note: Sometimes in this book the source code lines do not fit within the horizontal width and the right side of the code text on next line. Do not insert a new line character to duplicate what you see in the book, it should be all in one line.

# Chapter 2

## IntyBASIC setup

To start developing Intellivision games you need a machine running any of this software:

- Windows™ XP or better.
- Mac OS X 10.6 or better.
- Any recent Linux.

The most recent version of IntyBASIC is available at AtariAge using a very large URL address, but you can access it from my website http://nanochess.org/intybasic.html

This information assumes you're proficient using the command line, such as CMD in Windows and Terminal or shell in Mac or Linux.

You also need to download the jzintv emulator from http://spatula-city.org/~im14u2c/intv/ (don't forget to correctly select your platform between Windows, Mac or Linux)

After downloading the ZIP file for IntyBASIC, uncompress it in any folder. Same goes for jzintv.

Using the command line, navigate to your Documents folder:

- Windows: Access the Windows Start Menu, select Run, type "CMD" in the text field, press Enter and then type "cd my documents" followed by Enter, and then type "md intybasic" followed by Enter.

- Mac: Open a Terminal (you'll start in your home folder) and type "cd documents" followed by Enter, and then type "mkdir intybasic" followed by Enter.
- Linux: Open a shell window (you'll start in your home folder) and type "mkdir intybasic" followed by Enter.

Using the GUI interface to copy the compiler to your newly created folder. The required files are "*intybasic_prologue.asm*" and "*intybasic_epilogue.asm*" plus these ones:

- Windows: Copy IntyBASIC.exe and IntyColor.exe.
- Mac: Copy intybasic and intycolor.
- Linux: Copy intybasic_linux and intycolor_linux.

For Mac and Linux you may need to change the file permissions of executables, using "chmod 755 intybasic" for Mac and "chmod 755 intybasic_linux" for Linux.

Also copy the executables as1600 and jzintv from the jzintv package into the same folder. (as1600.exe, jzintv.exe, SDL.dll and libwinpthread-1.dll for Windows)

You'll need the Intellivision EXEC.ROM and GROM.ROM files that you can find on the Internet and copy them in that same folder.

Now that you're up and running, it's time to code your first IntyBASIC program.

If you're using Windows you can use Wordpad to type in your programs, just make sure to save your work as a "Text document" instead of RTF. Save as, and then in the Save as type box, choose all files. Then add ".bas" (without the quotes) to your file name. It should look like "filename.bas.*" as Windows tends to hide the file extension and will add ".txt" anyway. Always use extension ".bas" instead of ".txt" for all your source code files.

If you're using Mac OS X you can use TextEdit to type programs, select "Format/Convert to text" before saving with the extension ".bas" instead of ".txt".

For Linux you don't need guidelines because I assume you know how to use the "vi" or "vim" editors or other options like "emacs", "gedit", "nano" and "joe".

Also, on Windows, it is recommended to add the executable's directory to your PATH directive.

Your first program contains only two lines:

```
PRINT AT 0 COLOR 7,"Hello world!"
WHILE 1: WEND
```

Be sure to save the program as hello.bas and in the same folder where you copied the IntyBASIC compiler.

Then run the IntyBASIC compiler by entering the following command (don't forget to navigate to the folder using the "cd" command):

- Windows: intybasic hello.bas hello.asm

- Mac OS X: ./intybasic hello.bas hello.asm

- Linux: ./intybasic_linux hello.bas hello.asm

There's nothing else to do but wait. A brief text will appear to inform everything went right. For Mac OS X it could look like:

```
Aphrodite:intybook oscartoledo$ ./intybasic hello.bas hello.asm

IntyBASIC compiler v1.2.9 Nov/07/2017
(c) 2014-2016 Oscar Toledo G. http://nanochess.org/

0 used 8-bit variables of 228 available
0 used 16-bit variables of 47 available
Compilation finished

Aphrodite:intybook oscartoledo$
```

Then assemble the code:

- Windows: as1600 -o hello hello.asm

- Mac OS X: ./as1600 -o hello hello.asm

- Linux: ./as1600 -o hello hello.asm

And then run the emulator to test it:

- Windows: jzintv -z3 hello
- Mac OS X: ./jzintv -z3 hello
- Linux: ./jzintv -z3 hello

And voilà! A screen similar to this one should appear:

# Chapter 3

# Programming with IntyBASIC

Each line of the source file is executed sequentially by the Intellivision, until a decision statement is reached, then the execution flow can jump to another path.

Each source line can be composed of a label, an statement and a comment started with an apostrophe.

For example:

```
message: PRINT AT 5 COLOR 7,"Here" ' Comment.
         GOTO message
```

IntyBASIC functions by saving and reading information from variables and arrays (a table of consecutive values saved under a single name).

There are 2 types of values, namely 8-bit values (which can contain values from 0 to 255 or -128 to 127 if marked as *SIGNED*) and 16-bit values (which can contain values from -32768 to 32767 or 0 to 65535 if marked as *UNSIGNED*).

Variables and arrays of 8-bit data can be named with alphanumeric characters and also the underscore character (_). The 16-bit variables and arrays must always start with the character #.

Names and statements in IntyBASIC are case-insensitive, this means "a" and "A" represents the same variable, and "PRINT", "print" and "PrinT" means the same statement.

In this book, all statements and constants appears in uppercase, while variable names and other text appears in lowercase.

For example:

```
a = 255     ' Loads 255 into variable a
#a = 65535  ' Loads 65535 into #a
            ' This is a different variable from "a"!
```

The "=" symbol is the assignment operator. The left side indicates where to save the data, and the right side calculates the value to be saved. Pretty similar to a calculator.

```
a = 5
b = 7
c = a + b
d = a * b
```

The Intellivision has scarce memory so you can only have 240 8-bit variables and from 19 to 47 16-bits variables (depending on extensions selected, more on this later.)

Apart from the assignment operator there are statements to control execution flow and work with the video, sound and controllers.

These are the main statements composing the language (for a full list please consult the IntyBASIC manual available in appendix A):

```
REM
SIGNED
UNSIGNED
CONST

PROCEDURE/END
```

```
GOTO
GOSUB/RETURN
IF/THEN/ELSEIF/ELSE/END IF
FOR/NEXT
WHILE/WEND
DO WHILE/LOOP
DO UNTIL/LOOP
DO/LOOP WHILE
DO/LOOP UNTIL
EXIT FOR
EXIT WHILE
EXIT DO
ON GOTO/ON GOSUB

WAIT
DIM
RESTORE/READ/DATA
DEFINE
SOUND
SPRITE
CLS
PRINT
SCROLL
BORDER
MODE
SCREEN
BITMAP
PLAY
VOICE
DEF FN
INCLUDE
```

The expressions can use the following operators:

```
+             addition
-             substraction and negation operator
*             multiply
/             division
%             modulo
AND           logical AND
OR            logical OR
XOR           logical XOR
NOT           logical NOT
=             equal
<>            non-equal
```

```
<            less than
<=           less equal than
>            greater than
>=           greater equal than
ABS(expr)    absolute value
SGN(expr)    sign
CONT1        read controller 1
CONT2        read controller 2
COL0 - COL7  read collision bits
RAND         get a random number
RAND(range)  get a random number in a range
RANDOM(range) get a new random number in a range
FRAME        get current frame number
NTSC         indicates if Intellivision is NTSC
#backtab(expr) reads/writes screen
```

# 3.1 Our first IntyBASIC program

Now let us work on our first real IntyBASIC program.

```
    ' Example 1

    CLS ' Clears the screen
    DEFINE 5,1,smiling_face ' Define card 5 as a smiling face

    c = 0
main_loop:
    #backtab(c) = $0807 + 5 * 8 ' Place it on the screen
    WAIT ' Wait for a frame
    WAIT ' Wait for a frame
    WAIT ' Wait for a frame
    WAIT ' Wait for a frame
    WAIT ' Wait for a frame
    #backtab(c) = 0            ' Remove it from the screen
    c = c + 1                  ' Increase value of c by 1
    IF c = 240 THEN c = 0      ' If c equals 240 then make it zero
    GOTO main_loop

smiling_face:
    BITMAP "..XXXX.."
    BITMAP ".X....X."
    BITMAP "X.X..X.X"
    BITMAP "X......X"
```

```
BITMAP "X.X..X.X"
BITMAP "X..XX..X"
BITMAP ".X....X."
BITMAP "..XXXX.."
```

Now you can compile it and run it, a face moves over the screen.

Let's go over how this program works. It clears the screen using *CLS* and then defines our custom graphic using *DEFINE,* which points to *smiling_face* where a set of 8 *BITMAP* statements create the smiling face. Notice that each *BITMAP* statement contains 8 pixels between the quotes, the period marks a zero (no pixel) and the X marks a one (pixel drawn)

There is a variable *c* used to contain the current coordinate of the face. Its value runs from 0 to 239.

The face is loaded onto the screen using the *#backtab* array. This points to the screen composed of 20x12 cards (240 cards in total).

Intellivision screen (top left is card 0, bottom right is 239)

13

The value placed on screen requires a special format. In this case the value 2048 indicates to the Intellivision video processor to use one of the defined cards, the value 2048 can also be represented as $0800 (hexadecimal format).

To this value is added the number of the defined card (0 to 63, in this case 5) multiplied by 8, plus the number of the color to be used (7 in this case). The result is $0807.

These are the 16 colors of the Intellivision. The first 8 are considered the main colors:

| | |
|---|---|
| 0 - Black | 8 - Grey |
| 1 - Blue | 9 - Cyan |
| 2 - Red | 10 - Orange |
| 3 - Tan | 11 - Brown |
| 4 - Dark green | 12 - Pink |
| 5 - Green | 13 - Light blue |
| 6 - Yellow | 14 - Yellow green |
| 7 - White | 15 - Purple |

The upper 8 colors are available for display, but this depends on the current display mode (more on this later).

An important statement is *WAIT*, because it synchronizes the execution with the current frame display. This is important because some display events (like *DEFINE*, *BORDER* and *SPRITE*) happen only at the vertical blanking of the display.

In a NTSC Intellivision, *WAIT* synchronizes to the next 1/60th frame of display, while in a PAL Intellivision, it synchronizes to the next 1/50th frame of display.

Using 5 *WAIT* statements in a row is equivalent to waiting 1/12 of a second for NTSC or 1/10 of a second for PAL.

Then the code is repeated continuously by means of a *GOTO* statement that makes the flow to return to the *main_loop* label (marked by its name plus a colon character).

Notice how in this program the face moves abruptly in increments of 8 pixels, because each card measures 8x8 pixels.

Also notice that you can comment profusely your program, as these are ignored by the compiler and doesn't make slower your code.

## 3.2 Our first SPRITE

Let us replace the main loop of first program with this one:

```
main_loop:
    SPRITE 0, $0300 + c, $0100 + 8, $0807 + 5 * 8
    WAIT ' Wait for a frame
    WAIT ' Wait for a frame
    WAIT ' Wait for a frame
    WAIT ' Wait for a frame
    WAIT ' Wait for a frame
    c = c + 1             ' Increase value of c by 1
    IF c = 168 THEN c = 0   ' If c equals 168 then make it zero
    GOTO main_loop
```

Run it and voilà! The face moves in increments of one pixel across the screen.

We are now using one of the Intellivision video chip's (or STIC) special features, the sprites or MOBs (Movable OBject).

You can have up to 8 sprites at the same time on the screen (the sprite number is specified by the first argument of the *SPRITE* statement) and each one can be in a different position on the screen.

Notice the "magic" values *$0300* and *$0100*. The first one tells the Intellivision to enable the display of a sprite (*$0200*) and enables collision detection with other sprites (*$0100*); both added together gives a value of *$0300*.

The other value indicates that the card is 8x8 pixels in size.

The sprite coordinates are offset by 8 pixels, this allows a sprite to enter smoothly from the top edge of the screen and/or the left edge of the screen, also allows it to exit smoothly through the right and bottom edges of the screen.

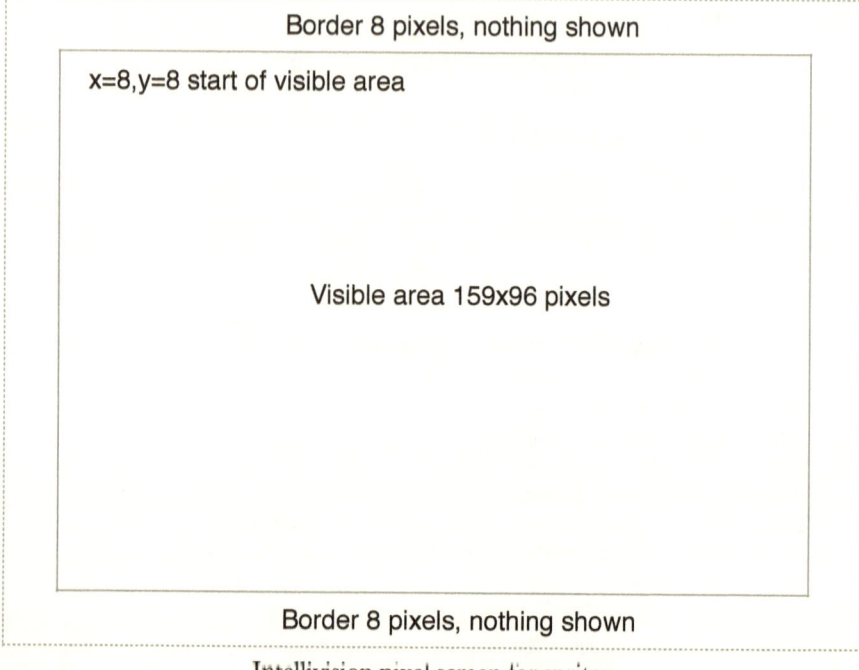

Intellivision pixel screen for sprites

And finally the fourth argument of SPRITE is used to choose the card bitmap to use as the sprite. This works the same way as when writing to *#backtab* (though it differs slightly, more on this later) and it includes the color value.

Notice how the sprite enters smoothly from the left side of the screen, being clipped automatically by the STIC, and the clipping also happens when exiting on the right side.

## 3.3 Controlling the game

So far we've done a repetitive task, now let us control the sprite using the Intellivision left controller.

The controllers weren't labeled as player 1 or 2, but as left and right. For IntyBASIC, the left controller can be accessed using *CONT1*, and the right controller using *CONT2*, or both controllers combined as *CONT*.

Let us use *CONT1* with the example program.

```
' Example 3

CLS  ' Clears the screen
DEFINE 5,1,smiling_face' Define card as a smiling face

x = 84
y = 52
main_loop:
    SPRITE 0, $0300 + x, $0100 + y, $0807 + 5 * 8
    WAIT ' Wait for a frame
    IF cont1.up THEN y = y - 1
    IF cont1.down THEN y = y + 1
    IF cont1.left THEN x = x - 1
    IF cont1.right THEN x = x + 1
    GOTO main_loop

smiling_face:
    BITMAP "..XXXX.."
    BITMAP ".X....X."
    BITMAP "X.X..X.X"
    BITMAP "X......X"
    BITMAP "X.X..X.X"
    BITMAP "X..XX..X"
    BITMAP ".X....X."
    BITMAP "..XXXX.."
```

Compile it, then run it.

Now you can move the happy face using the left controller.

The *IF* statement is used with an expression in this case to read the left controller directions and direct it to change the coordinates of the face.

However there is a problem, the face can go off the screen. Let us limit the range of movement to make it elegant.

```
IF cont1.up THEN IF y > 8 THEN y = y - 1
IF cont1.down THEN IF y < 96 THEN y = y + 1
```

```
IF cont1.left THEN IF x > 8 THEN x = x - 1
IF cont1.right THEN IF x < 160 THEN x = x + 1
```

You can compile and run it now and see how the face is limited to the borders of the screen. As a side note, when moving the face all the way to the right, you'll see how a pixel is missing. This is because the Intellivision doesn't show the 160th pixel on the right side of the screen.

Notice how we are using an *IF* statement inside another *IF* statement.

Another way of writing the *IF* statement is like this:

```
IF cont1.up THEN
    IF y > 8 THEN y = y - 1
END IF
IF cont1.down THEN
    IF y < 96 THEN y = y + 1
END IF
IF cont1.left THEN
    IF x > 8 THEN x = x - 1
END IF
IF cont1.right THEN
    IF x < 160 THEN x = x + 1
END IF
```

This is a block usage where the inner statements can be as long as required and *END IF* marks the end of the block. You can use as many *IF/ END IF* as you want.

If you want to use the right controller then you can replace *cont1* with *cont2*. Or replace it with *CONT* (without a number) in order to move the face with any of the two controllers.

## 3.4 Add a title screen

Let us add a title screen for this "game" using this code at the start.

```
CLS
```

```
PRINT AT 44 COLOR 7,"Smiling face"

PRINT AT 202 COLOR 6,"Press any button"

DO
     WAIT
     c = CONT1
LOOP WHILE c

DO
     WAIT
     c = CONT1
LOOP WHILE c = 0
```

The statement *PRINT* is used to display text and numbers. In this case, the *AT* idiom indicates the card position where the text will begin, the *COLOR* idiom indicates the color to be used and then the string is translated automatically to GROM characters to be displayed.

This code uses a repetitive loop. In this case, *DO* marks the start of the loop and *LOOP WHILE* indicates the condition that will cause the loop to continue until the condition evaluates to "false".

In essence, each loop can be rewritten with *IF* and *GOTO* like this for the last loop.

```
repetition:
     WAIT
     c = CONT1
     IF c = 0 THEN GOTO repetition
```

Again, I recommend going over the available statements in the IntyBASIC manual where each one is described in greater detail (check Appendix A).

## 3.5 Sound

We've seen how to control graphics, some color, the controllers and now let us examine how to output sound.

The sound chip AY-3-8914 is the predecessor to the AY-3-8910 PSG (Programmable Sound Generator). Both have three tone channels and a noise channel that can be mixed with each tone channel.

Each tone channel also has an independent volume level and a shared volume envelope that allows for interesting effects. You can search on Internet for the AY-3-8914 datasheet for more information, or check Appendix B.

Now for some music theory: The A note basic to all music is 440 hz. In order to generate this frequency or calculate the tone value for a frequency, we need to follow this formula (change 3579545 to 4000000 if you have a PAL Intellivision):

$$period = 3579545 / 32 / frequency$$

$$254.2 = 3579545 / 32 / 440$$

Now to play it, we use:

```
SOUND 0,254,10
```

The 10 specifies the volume for the channel, which can be 0 for silence (default) to 15 (highest volume), but typically the Intellivision hardware volume is too high, so 13, 14 and 15 all sound like the highest volume.

Let us try it in a separate program:

```
SOUND 0,254,10
WHILE 1: WEND
```

The *WHILE* statement repeats the internal loop while the expression is non-zero, so since the expression is simply "1", this is an infinite loop. The internal statement block ends with the *WEND* keyword.

Also notice the colon character; this symbol is a separator that allows multiple statements on the same line, in this case *WHILE* and *WEND*. Both could be rewritten as:

```
WHILE 1
WEND
```

And the end result would be the same. This should not be confused with labels that are names at the start of lines terminated with a single colon.

But running this program demonstrates a problem, it's a non-stopping tone!

Let us try this:

```
WHILE 1
      FOR c = 0 TO 50
            WAIT
            SOUND 0,,0
      NEXT c
      FOR c = 0 TO 10
            WAIT
            SOUND 0,254,10
      NEXT c
WEND
```

This plays the tone each second for 1/10th of a second (in a NTSC console), and it sounds like a heart beat in a machine.

Notice the usage of the *FOR* statement, which assigns a value to a variable and then counts up to the number specified after *TO*.

Also notice the idiom *SOUND 0,,0* which means to change only the volume to zero, the second argument is left blank. We only need to turn the volume to zero to turn off a channel, there is no need to change the frequency.

Let us play with the channel volume:

```
WHILE 1
    FOR c = 0 TO 50
        WAIT
        SOUND 0,,0
    NEXT c
    FOR c = 0 TO 10
        WAIT
        SOUND 0,254,10-c
    NEXT c
WEND
```

Now it sounds somewhat like a bell because of the decaying sound. Now let us play with the frequency:

```
WHILE 1
    FOR c = 0 TO 50
        WAIT
        SOUND 0,,0
    NEXT c
    FOR c = 0 TO 10
        WAIT
        SOUND 0,254-c*5,10-c
    NEXT c
WEND
```

Well this is now an arcade-esque sound effect.

Let us try the three sound channels.

```
WHILE 1
    FOR c = 0 TO 40
        WAIT
        SOUND 0,,0
        SOUND 1,,0
        SOUND 2,,0
    NEXT c
    FOR c = 0 TO 20
```

```
         WAIT
         SOUND 0,254-c*5,10-c/2
         SOUND 1,127+c*3,10-c/2
         SOUND 2,508-c*10,10-c/2
      NEXT c
WEND
```

This is only an example of the capabilities of the sound chip.

IntyBASIC also provides a music tracker that can play pretty complex music with pre-generated "instruments", but with an important caveat, it also uses the sound channels. Fortunately, it provides methods to define music while leaving a free channel for sound effects (for example).

```
CLS
PRINT AT 22 COLOR 6,"Twinkle, Twinkle"
PRINT AT 44,"Little Star"

PRINT AT 182 COLOR 5,"Press controller"
PRINT AT 206,"to start"

DO
      WAIT
      c = CONT1
LOOP WHILE c

DO
      WAIT
      c = CONT1
LOOP WHILE c = 0

PLAY SIMPLE
PLAY twinkle_twinkle_little_star

CLS
WHILE 1
      c = RANDOM(240)
      PRINT AT c COLOR 7,"."
      FOR d = 0 TO 20
          WAIT
      NEXT d
      PRINT AT c," "
WEND

twinkle_twinkle_little_star:
```

```
DATA 20

MUSIC D4,-,-
MUSIC D4,-,-
MUSIC A4,-,-
MUSIC A4,-,-

MUSIC B4,-,-
MUSIC B4,-,-
MUSIC A4,-,-
MUSIC S,-,-

MUSIC G4,-,-
MUSIC G4,-,-
MUSIC F4#,-,-
MUSIC F4#,-,-

MUSIC E4,-,-
MUSIC E4,-,-
MUSIC D4,-,-
MUSIC S,-,-

MUSIC A4,-,-
MUSIC A4,-,-
MUSIC G4,-,-
MUSIC G4,-,-

MUSIC F4#,-,-
MUSIC F4#,-,-
MUSIC E4,-,-
MUSIC S,-,-

MUSIC A4,-,-
MUSIC A4,-,-
MUSIC G4,-,-
MUSIC G4,-,-

MUSIC F4#,-,-
MUSIC F4#,-,-
MUSIC E4,-,-
MUSIC S,-,-

MUSIC D4,-,-
MUSIC D4,-,-
MUSIC A4,-,-
MUSIC A4,-,-

MUSIC B4,-,-
```

```
MUSIC B4,-,-
MUSIC A4,-,-
MUSIC S,-,-

MUSIC G4,-,-
MUSIC G4,-,-
MUSIC F4#,-,-
MUSIC F4#,-,-

MUSIC E4,-,-
MUSIC E4,-,-
MUSIC D4,-,-
MUSIC S,-,-

MUSIC STOP
```

The new thing here is the *PLAY* statement that lets the programmer select the tracker mode and the music track to play. The *MUSIC* statement contains the notes (up to 3 channels) and the *MUSIC STOP* statement indicates when to stop playing music. Also implemented is *MUSIC REPEAT* when we want the music to loop endlessly.

Also notice the usage of the *RANDOM* expression which generates a value between 0 to 239, which is used as the card number to display a dot, suggesting a star. We then wait a little and erase the star.

IntyBASIC keeps playing the music in the background by itself without further interaction.

You can see in the compilation report that IntyBASIC uses extra variables for the music player.

# Chapter 4

# A Game of Ball

For our first significant programming assignment, let us start with a classic game where a pair of paddles hit a ball.

There is a border for the game field and a separator in the middle, also a scoreboard for each player.

The rules are simple: Both players move their paddle up and down, and if the ball exits the screen behind a paddle, the opponent scores one point.

## 4.1 Setting up the graphics

Let us start by setting up the graphics and clearing the screen:

```
'
' Game of Ball
' by Oscar Toledo G.
' Creation date: Jun/11/2018.
'

CLS
MODE 0,0,0,0,0
WAIT
DEFINE 0,7,game_bitmaps_0
WAIT

WHILE 1: WEND ' Infinite loop

'
```

```
     ' Graphics for borders of playfield, paddles and ball.
     '
game_bitmaps_0:
     BITMAP "11111111"
     BITMAP "11111111"
     BITMAP "00000000"
     BITMAP "00000000"
     BITMAP "00000000"
     BITMAP "00000000"
     BITMAP "00000000"
     BITMAP "00000000"

     BITMAP "00000000"
     BITMAP "00000000"
     BITMAP "00000000"
     BITMAP "00000000"
     BITMAP "00000000"
     BITMAP "00000000"
     BITMAP "11111111"
     BITMAP "11111111"

     BITMAP "11111111"
     BITMAP "11111111"
     BITMAP "00000000"
     BITMAP "00000001"
     BITMAP "00000001"
     BITMAP "00000000"
     BITMAP "00000000"
     BITMAP "00000001"

     BITMAP "00000001"
     BITMAP "00000000"
     BITMAP "00000000"
     BITMAP "00000001"
     BITMAP "00000001"
     BITMAP "00000000"
     BITMAP "00000000"
     BITMAP "00000001"

     BITMAP "00000001"
     BITMAP "00000000"
     BITMAP "00000000"
     BITMAP "00000001"
     BITMAP "00000001"
     BITMAP "00000000"
     BITMAP "11111111"
     BITMAP "11111111"
```

```
BITMAP "11000000"
BITMAP "11000000"
BITMAP "11000000"
BITMAP "11000000"
BITMAP "11000000"
BITMAP "11000000"
BITMAP "11000000"
BITMAP "11000000"

BITMAP "11000000"
BITMAP "11000000"
BITMAP "00000000"
BITMAP "00000000"
BITMAP "00000000"
BITMAP "00000000"
BITMAP "00000000"
BITMAP "00000000"
```

Notice how bitmaps are defined in terms of ones and zeros this time, but these could be replaced by "X" and "." with no change in behavior.

Running this program will generate a blank screen but behind the scenes the Intellivision GRAM now contains 7 graphics of 8x8 pixels to draw the borders of the playfield, the ball and the paddles.

## 4.2 Drawing the playfield

Let us draw the playfield (adding this code just before the infinite loop)

```
'
' Draw the playfield
'
CLS

PRINT AT 0 COLOR 1
FOR c = 1 TO 20
PRINT "\256"
NEXT c

PRINT AT 220
FOR c = 1 to 20
PRINT "\257"
```

```
    NEXT c

    PRINT AT 9, "\258"

    FOR c = 1 TO 10
    PRINT AT c * 20 + 9, "\259"
    NEXT c

    PRINT AT 229, "\260"

    GOSUB update_score
```

This code draws the playfield. But we added something new here, namely a call to a subroutine. This code won't compile unless we add the subroutine and we'll add it after the infinite loop (*WHILE 1: WEND*).

```
    '
    ' Update score for both players
    '
update_score:   PROCEDURE
    ' Show score at 2 digits aligned to right
    PRINT AT 27 COLOR 1,<.2>score1
    ' Show score as digits aligned to left
    PRINT AT 31 COLOR 2,<>score2
    END
```

We're now using a feature of the *PRINT* statement to show numbers, which takes the integer value passed to it (*score1* and *score2*) and transforms it to the internal GROM characters of the Intellivision meant to represent decimal digits. The color is also specified.

Once we compile and run the game, we get a game screen.

Now we're seeing something recognizable.

# 4.3 Paddles

Let us add the paddles for playing the game. After *GOSUB update_score* add this code:

```
x1 = 23
y1 = 42
x2 = 137
y2 = 42
```

Now replace the *WHILE 1: WEND* with this code:

```
'
' Main game loop
'
ball_loop:
    WAIT

    SPRITE 0, $0708 + x1, $0208 + y1, $0800 + 5 * 8 + 1
    SPRITE 1, $0708 + x2, $0208 + y2, $0800 + 5 * 8 + 2

    IF cont1.up THEN IF y1 > 6 THEN y1 = y1 - 2
    IF cont1.down THEN IF y1 < 74 THEN y1 = y1 + 2

    IF cont2.up THEN IF y2 > 6 THEN y2 = y2 - 2
    IF cont2.down THEN IF y2 < 74 THEN y2 = y2 + 2

    GOTO ball_loop
```

This gets us a screen where paddles appear and can be moved using the left and right controllers.

We're using two sprites this time, and this code is very similar to the code we used before for moving a face over the screen, including limits so the paddles don't go beyond the screen borders.

## 4.4 The ball

Now we can add the ball. This code is to be inserted after *y2 = 42*

```
GOSUB restart_ball
x = ox
y = oy
#dx = -2
#dy = -2
ball_speed = $20
ball_current = 0
```

This code is to be inserted before *IF CONT1.UP*

```
IF ball = 0 THEN
     SPRITE 2, 0
ELSE
     SPRITE 2, $0708 + x, $0208 + y, $0800 + 6 * 8 + 6
END IF
```

And this code is to be inserted before *GOTO ball_loop*

```
IF ball THEN

    ball_current = ball_current + ball_speed
    IF ball_current >= $40 THEN

        ball_current = ball_current - $40

        ox = x
        oy = y
        x = x + #dx
        y = y + #dy

        IF oy + #dy < 2 THEN
            #dy = -#dy
            oy = 2 - #dy
            GOSUB ball
        END IF
```

```
                    IF oy + #dy > 90 THEN
                        #dy = -#dy
                        oy = 90 - #dy
                        GOSUB ball
                    END IF
                    IF ox + #dx < 2 THEN
                        GOSUB ball_out
                        GOSUB restart_ball
                    END IF
                    IF ox + #dx > 158 THEN
                        GOSUB ball_out
                        GOSUB restart_ball
                    END IF

                    IF x > x1 - 4 AND x < x1 + 4 THEN
                        c = y1
                        GOSUB rebound
                    END IF
                    IF x > x2 - 4 AND x < x2 + 4 THEN
                        c = y2
                        GOSUB rebound
                    END IF

                    x = ox + #dx
                    y = oy + #dy
                END IF
        ELSE
            c = cont AND $E0
            IF (c = $a0) + (c = $c0) + (c = $60) THEN ball = 1
        END IF
```

And we also need some support code (add after *GOTO ball_loop*):

```
        '
        ' Ball touched wall
        '
ball:   PROCEDURE
        END

        '
        ' Ball went out of field
        '
ball_out:   PROCEDURE
        IF x < 80 THEN
            score2 = score2 + 1
        ELSE
```

```
            score1 = score1 + 1
        END IF
        GOSUB update_score
        END


        '
        ' Restart the ball
        '
restart_ball: PROCEDURE
        d = RAND % 8
        ox = 80
        oy = 48
        ball = 0
        GOSUB get_angle
        END


        '
        ' Rebound procedure
        ' Check if ball hits paddle (y coordinate, x already checked)
        '
rebound: PROCEDURE
        IF y < c - 3 THEN RETURN
        IF y > c + 15 THEN RETURN
        IF y < c THEN
            d = 0
        ELSE
            d = (y - c) / 2
        END IF
        GOSUB get_angle
        IF ball_speed < $40 THEN ball_speed = ball_speed + 1
        END


        '
        ' Get angle per paddle position
        ' Variable d contains the hit position.
        ' Returns dx and dy with new direction.
        '
get_angle:    PROCEDURE
        IF d = 0 THEN #dy = -2:IF #dx < 0 THEN #dx = 1 ELSE #dx = -1
        IF d = 1 THEN #dy = -2:IF #dx < 0 THEN #dx = 2 ELSE #dx = -2
        IF d = 2 THEN #dy = -1:IF #dx < 0 THEN #dx = 2 ELSE #dx = -2
        IF d = 3 THEN #dy = 0:IF #dx < 0 THEN #dx = 2 ELSE #dx = -2
        IF d = 4 THEN #dy = 0:IF #dx < 0 THEN #dx = 2 ELSE #dx = -2
        IF d = 5 THEN #dy = 1:IF #dx < 0 THEN #dx = 2 ELSE #dx = -2
        IF d = 6 THEN #dy = 2:IF #dx < 0 THEN #dx = 2 ELSE #dx = -2
        IF d = 7 THEN #dy = 2:IF #dx < 0 THEN #dx = 1 ELSE #dx = -1
        END
```

How does this works? Essentially the ball position is contained in variables *x* and *y*, and the current direction goes into variables *#dx* and *#dy*. We also have the current speed of the ball in variable *ball_speed*, and if the ball is active in variable *ball* (non-zero or zero for inactive).

The ball is enabled by pressing one of the side-buttons of the controllers. Once the ball is enabled, *ball_current* increases with the current speed (*ball_speed*) and after crossing the value of $40 (64 in decimal), it moves the ball in its current direction.

This means the ball can move by fractional positions, making it smoother to the player's eyes.

Before moving the *x,y* coordinates of the ball, we save the current position in *ox,oy*.

The program checks for a collision against the top and bottom wall. (*oy + #dy < 2* and *oy + #dy > 90*)

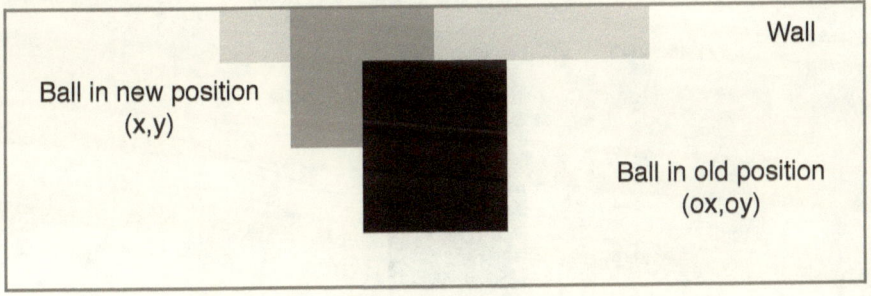

Ball before hitting wall in case oy + #dy < 2

Then it checks for the ball exiting by the left and right sides. (*ox + #dx < 2* and *ox + #dx > 158*)

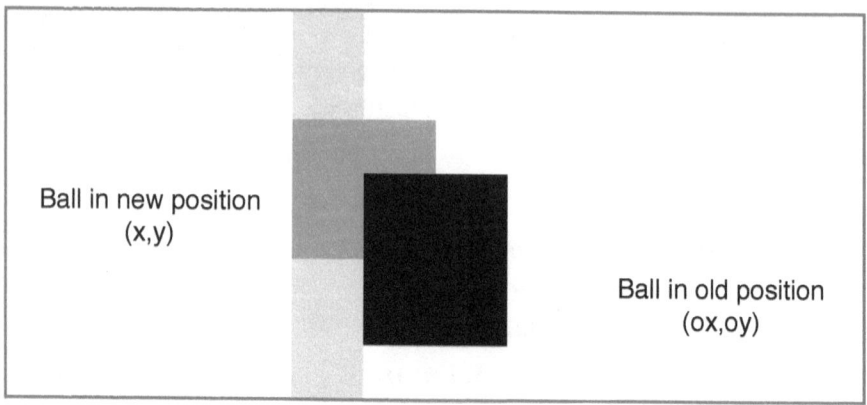

Ball before exiting screen in case ox + #dx < 2

And finally it checks if the ball crosses the X coordinate of one of the paddles (checking for $x > x1 - 4$ and $x < x1 + 4$). Notice that the ball is slightly "fat" so there is a range to check.

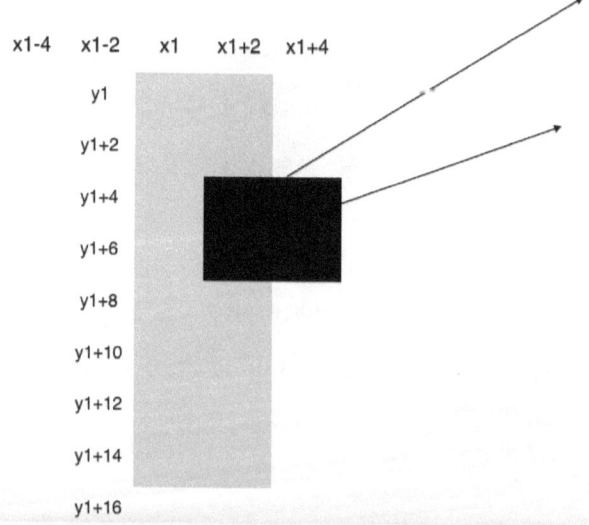

This check isn't enough, the vertical position is going to be considered by the subroutine for rebound purposes ($y < c - 3$ or $y > c + 15$ means the ball didn't touch the paddle).

If the ball hits a paddle, then there are 8 directions which can be chosen for the ball based on the vertical position of the collision.

# 4.5 Sound

The game plays really well, the ball speeds up every time it gets hit, the paddles have fast reaction, the ball can become unpredictable. But, the game is as silent as outer space.

It's time to add some sound effects.

First, we create some code to disable a sound effect after a small interval. This is to be put after the line saying *WAIT* after the *game_loop:* label

```
IF sound_counter > 0 THEN
    sound_counter = sound_counter - 1
    IF sound_counter = 0 THEN SOUND 2, 1, 0
END IF
```

There is an empty procedure called *ball*. Let us replace it with the code for making the bouncing sound when it touches the top or bottom walls.

```
'
' Ball touched wall
'
ball:    PROCEDURE
    SOUND 2,500,48
    SOUND 3,400,9
    sound_counter = 10
    END
```

For the procedure *ball_out*, just before the line saying *END*, add this code:

```
SOUND 2,330,48
SOUND 3,70,10
sound_counter = 15
```

And finally in the *rebound* procedure before the line saying *END*, add this code:

```
SOUND 2,150,48
SOUND 3,300,9
sound_counter = 5
```

And now the game is complete with sounds.

We're using channel 2 for sound effects. Notice the value 48 for the volume, which means we use a *volume envelope* whose frequency and duration is controlled by *SOUND 3* (the first value is the frequency and the next one is the type of envelope on the AY-3-8914, which is documented in appendix B).

Feel free to experiment with this game. For example, how about adding a second ball? or adding walls to the left and right sides?

Can your logical mind derive the required code?

It's a challenge like everything in life.

# Chapter 5

## Monkey Moon

In this programming assignment, let us reinvent a classic not mentioned by name, but you can guess how I came up with the name.

The story is more or less as follows: Your astronaut is stranded on the moon, but it happens to be the Monkey Moon, where a giant monkey rules. He's not very happy with your visit, so he throws giant moon stones at you. Your objective is to reach the top to move on to the next level.

## 5.1 Planning

This time we'll use animated graphics. We have the following animated things on screen:

- Rock (2 frames, using Intellivision hardware we'll generate 2 extra frames using X and Y mirroring)
- Player (4 frames, 2 of these for walking, 1 for going up/down ladders and 1 for death)

Also we'll need the following fixed graphics:

- Girders. (5 cards)
- Lunar monkey (4 cards for body, 1 for face in another color)

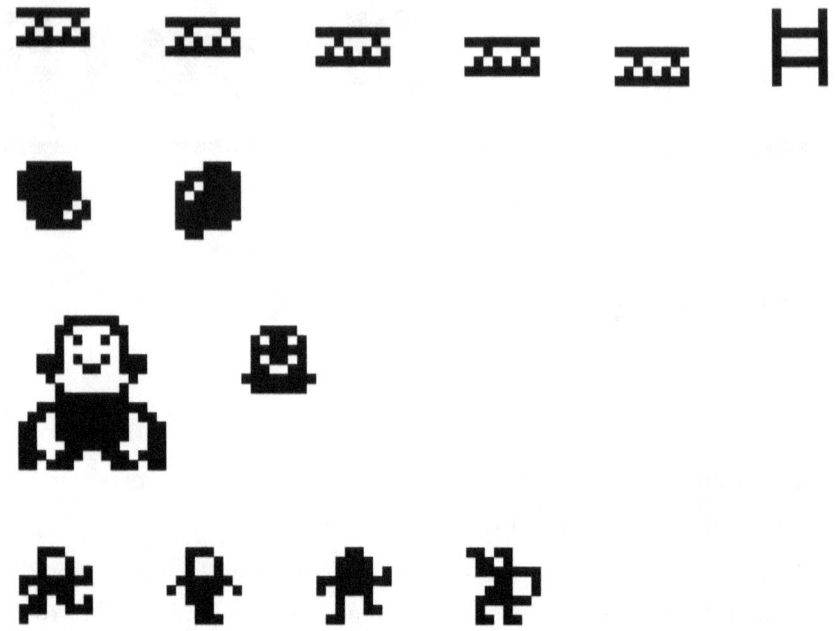

## 5.2 Code for graphics

This is the code to define the graphics for the game:

```
      '
      ' Monkey moon
      ' by Oscar Toledo G.
      ' Creation date: Jun/11/2018.
      '

      CLS
      MODE 0,0,0,0,0
      WAIT
      DEFINE 0,16,game_bitmaps_0
      WAIT
      DEFINE 16,1,game_bitmaps_1
      WAIT
start_game:

      WHILE 1: WEND

      '
      ' Bitmaps for the game (first section)
```

```
'
game_bitmaps_0:
    BITMAP "XXXXXXXX"    ' 0
    BITMAP "..X...X."
    BITMAP ".X.X.X.X"
    BITMAP "XXXXXXXX"
    BITMAP "........"
    BITMAP "........"
    BITMAP "........"
    BITMAP "........"

    BITMAP "........"    ' 1
    BITMAP "XXXXXXXX"
    BITMAP "..X...X."
    BITMAP ".X.X.X.X"
    BITMAP "XXXXXXXX"
    BITMAP "........"
    BITMAP "........"
    BITMAP "........"

    BITMAP "........"    ' 2
    BITMAP "........"
    BITMAP "XXXXXXXX"
    BITMAP "..X...X."
    BITMAP ".X.X.X.X"
    BITMAP "XXXXXXXX"
    BITMAP "........"
    BITMAP "........"

    BITMAP "........"    ' 3
    BITMAP "........"
    BITMAP "........"
    BITMAP "XXXXXXXX"
    BITMAP "..X...X."
    BITMAP ".X.X.X.X"
    BITMAP "XXXXXXXX"
    BITMAP "........"

    BITMAP "........"    ' 4
    BITMAP "........"
    BITMAP "........"
    BITMAP "........"
    BITMAP "XXXXXXXX"
    BITMAP "..X...X."
    BITMAP ".X.X.X.X"
    BITMAP "XXXXXXXX"

    BITMAP ".X....X."    ' 5
```

41

```
BITMAP ".X....X."
BITMAP ".XXXXX."
BITMAP ".X....X."
BITMAP ".X....X."
BITMAP ".XXXXX."
BITMAP ".X....X."
BITMAP ".X....X."

BITMAP ".XXXXX.."    ' 6
BITMAP "XXXXXXX."
BITMAP "XXXXXXX."
BITMAP "XXXXXXX."
BITMAP ".XXXXX.X"
BITMAP ".XXXX.XX"
BITMAP "..XXXXX."
BITMAP "........"

BITMAP "....XXX."    ' 7
BITMAP "..XXXXXX"
BITMAP ".XX.XXXX"
BITMAP ".X.XXXXX"
BITMAP ".XXXXXXX"
BITMAP ".XXXXXXX"
BITMAP ".XXXXXX."
BITMAP "..XX...."

BITMAP "........"    ' 8
BITMAP "..XXXX.."
BITMAP ".X.XX.X."
BITMAP ".XXXXXX."
BITMAP ".X.XX.X."
BITMAP ".XX..XX."
BITMAP "XXXXXXXX"
BITMAP ".XXXXXX."

BITMAP ".....XXX"    ' 9
BITMAP "....XX.."
BITMAP "....X.X."
BITMAP "....X..."
BITMAP "..XXX.X."
BITMAP "..XXX..X"
BITMAP "...X...."
BITMAP "....X..."
BITMAP "....XXXX"    ' 10
BITMAP "..XXXXXX"
BITMAP ".XX.XXXX"
BITMAP "XX..XXXX"
BITMAP "XX..XXXX"
```

```
BITMAP "XX...XXX"
BITMAP "XXX.XXX."
BITMAP "XX.XXX.."

BITMAP "XXX....."  ' 11
BITMAP "..XX...."
BITMAP ".X.X...."
BITMAP "...X...."
BITMAP ".X.XXX.."
BITMAP "X..XXX.."
BITMAP "....X..."
BITMAP "...X...."
BITMAP "XXXX...."  ' 12
BITMAP "XXXXXX.."
BITMAP "XXXX.XX."
BITMAP "XXXX..XX"
BITMAP "XXXX..XX"
BITMAP "XXX...XX"
BITMAP ".XXX.XXX"
BITMAP "..XXX.XX"

BITMAP "..XXX..."  ' 13
BITMAP "..X..X.."
BITMAP "..X..X.X"
BITMAP "XXXXXXXX"
BITMAP "X.XXXX.."
BITMAP ".XX.XX.X"
BITMAP "XXX..XXX"
BITMAP "X......."

BITMAP "..XXX..."  ' 14
BITMAP "..X..X.."
BITMAP "..X..X.."
BITMAP ".XXXXXX."
BITMAP "X.XXXX.X"
BITMAP "..XXX..."
BITMAP "...XX..."
BITMAP "...XXX.."

BITMAP "...XX..."  ' 15
BITMAP "..XXXX.."
BITMAP "..XXXX.X"
BITMAP "XXXXXXXX"
BITMAP "X.XXXX.."
BITMAP "..X..X.."
BITMAP "..X..XX."
BITMAP ".XX....."
```

```
'
' Bitmaps for the game (second section)
'
game_bitmaps_1:
    BITMAP "XX.XX..."  ' 16
    BITMAP ".XX.X..."
    BITMAP ".XXXXXXX"
    BITMAP "...XX..X"
    BITMAP "..XXX..X"
    BITMAP ".XXXXX."
    BITMAP ".X..X..."
    BITMAP ".XX.XX.."
```

Notice how we used two *DEFINE* statements to load the graphics, intermixed with *WAIT* statements. This is because the Intellivision can only load 16 defined cards during each video frame.

## 5.3 The level

Now we need the prepare the screen with the defined graphics. This will be a screen of platforms and ladders, with the monkey at the top and rocks at the top right corner. Also we'll reserve some space for the score, bonus and lives indicators.

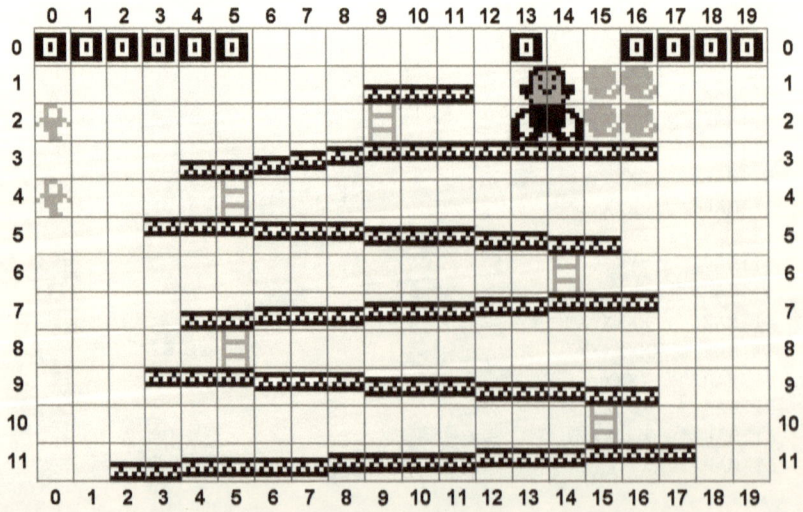

In order to integrate this screen into the game, we'll use a new statement of IntyBASIC: *CONST*. This statement allows us to assign a name to a constant, so instead of using the constant we'll use the name.

This is to be inserted before the *CLS* statement.

```
CONST MOB_LEFT = $0308  ' Enabled + interact + hidden border
CONST MOB_TOP = $0108   ' Normal size + hidden border
CONST MIRROR_X = $0400  ' Sprite reflected in X direction
CONST MIRROR_Y = $0800  ' Sprite reflected in Y direction

CONST OO = 0
CONST GA = $0801 + 0 * 8
CONST GB = $0801 + 1 * 8
CONST GC = $0801 + 2 * 8
CONST GD = $0801 + 3 * 8
CONST GE = $0801 + 4 * 8
CONST LA = $0805 + 5 * 8
CONST RA = $0802 + 6 * 8
CONST RB = $0802 + 7 * 8
CONST MF = $0806 + 8 * 8      ' Monkey face
CONST MA = $0802 + 9 * 8
CONST MB = $0802 + 10 * 8
CONST MC = $0802 + 11 * 8
CONST MD = $0802 + 12 * 8
CONST PA = $0807 + 14 * 8
CONST PB = $0807 + 13 * 8
CONST PC = $0807 + 15 * 8
CONST PD = $0807 + 16 * 8
```

The 2 letters names for the constants are using an initial letter which allows us to identify the graphic (G for Girder, L for Ladder, R for Rock and M for Monkey)

And now we use these constants for defining the screen adding this at the end of source code:

```
level1_cards:
    DATA 00,00,00,00,00,00,00,00,00,00,00,00,00,00,00,00,00,00,00,00
    DATA 00,00,00,00,00,00,00,00,00,GE,GE,GE,00,MA,MC,RA,RA,00,00,00
    DATA 00,00,00,00,00,00,00,00,00,LA,00,00,00,MB,MD,RA,RA,00,00,00
    DATA 00,00,00,00,GE,GE,GD,GC,GB,GA,GA,GA,GA,GA,GA,GA,GA,00,00,00
    DATA 00,00,00,00,00,LA,00,00,00,00,00,00,00,00,00,00,00,00,00,00
    DATA 00,00,00,GA,GA,GA,GB,GB,GB,GC,GC,GC,GD,GD,GE,GE,00,00,00,00
    DATA 00,00,00,00,00,00,00,00,00,00,00,00,00,00,LA,00,00,00,00,00
    DATA 00,00,00,00,GE,GE,GD,GD,GD,GC,GC,GC,GB,GB,GA,GA,GA,00,00,00
    DATA 00,00,00,00,00,LA,00,00,00,00,00,00,00,00,00,00,00,00,00,00
    DATA 00,00,00,GA,GA,GA,GB,GB,GB,GC,GC,GC,GD,GD,GD,GE,GE,00,00,00
    DATA 00,00,00,00,00,00,00,00,00,00,00,00,00,00,00,LA,00,00,00,00
    DATA 00,00,GE,GE,GD,GD,GD,GD,GC,GC,GC,GC,GB,GB,GB,GA,GA,GA,00,00
```

Thanks to the clever naming of constants, we can almost "see" the level in the data.

We're now using the *DATA* statement, which tells IntyBASIC that its content is to be saved as sequential numbers and can be accessed via several features of the language, like *SCREEN* which, in its simplest form, copies 240 numbers directly to the screen.

Before the *WHILE 1: WEND* line, insert this code:

```
restart_level:
    CLS
    SCREEN level1_cards
    FOR c = 0 TO 6
        SPRITE c, 0
    NEXT c
    SPRITE 7,MOB_LEFT + 13 * 8 + 4,MOB_TOP + 1 * 8, MF
```

Notice the *SCREEN* statement, which copies the data pointed by *level1_cards* directly into the screen. This is enough to see the level on the TV screen.

Also notice the use of *SPRITE 7* to put color placing it on the monkey face as the STIC doesn't allow more than 2 colors per 8x8 card, but extra color is added with the MOB.

## 5.4 The player

You can't do much with a static screen, it's like a demo. We want a player character object that can move around the screen.

This player object will use the *player_x* and *player_y* variables to manage its position on the screen, and *player_state* to manage its state (walking, going up/down over ladders, etc.) in order to show the correct graphic frame for the sprite.

Add the following, replacing *WHILE 1: WEND*

```
    player_x = 16
    player_y = 80
    player_state = 0

game_loop:
    x = player_x
    y = player_y
    IF player_state <> 2 AND player_state <> 6 THEN
        GOSUB get_offset
        player_offset = offset_y
    ELSE
        offset_y = 0
        player_offset = 0
    END IF
    IF player_state = 0 THEN
        SPRITE 0,MOB_LEFT + player_x, MOB_TOP + player_y +
offset_y, PA
    ELSEIF player_state = 1 THEN
        SPRITE 0,MOB_LEFT + player_x, MOB_TOP + player_y +
offset_y, PB
    ELSEIF player_state = 2 THEN
        SPRITE 0,MOB_LEFT + player_x, MOB_TOP + player_y +
offset_y, PC
    ELSEIF player_state = 4 THEN
        SPRITE 0,MOB_LEFT + player_x, MOB_TOP + MIRROR_X + player_y
+ offset_y, PA
    ELSEIF player_state = 5 THEN
        SPRITE 0,MOB_LEFT + player_x, MOB_TOP + MIRROR_X + player_y
+ offset_y, PB
    ELSEIF player_state = 6 THEN
        SPRITE 0,MOB_LEFT + player_x, MOB_TOP + MIRROR_X + player_y
+ offset_y, PC
    END IF
```

```
    WAIT

    c = CONT
    d = c AND $E0
    IF (d = $80) + (d = $40) + (d = $20) THEN
        ' Keypad pressed
    ELSEIF (d = $60) + (d = $a0) + (d = $c0) THEN   ' Side button
        ' Side button pressed
    ELSE
        d = controller_direction(c AND $1F)

        IF d = 2 THEN ' Going right
            IF player_y % 16 = 0 THEN     ' Only if aligned over
girder
                platform = player_y / 8 / 2
                IF player_x < max_platform(platform) THEN
                    sound_effect = 1: sound_state = 0
                    player_x = player_x + 1
                    IF player_state <> 0 AND player_state <> 1
THEN
                        player_state = 0
                    ELSEIF (FRAME AND 3) = 0 THEN
                        player_state = player_state XOR 1
                    END IF
                END IF
            END IF
        END IF
        IF d = 4 THEN ' Going left
            IF player_y % 16 = 0 THEN     ' Only if aligned over
girder
                platform = player_y / 8 / 2
                IF player_x > min_platform(platform) THEN
                    sound_effect = 1: sound_state = 0
                    player_x = player_x - 1
                    IF player_state <> 4 AND player_state <> 5
THEN
                        player_state = 4
                    ELSEIF (FRAME AND 3) = 0 THEN
                        player_state = player_state XOR 1
                    END IF
                END IF
            END IF
        END IF
    END IF

    GOTO game_loop
```

We have a new statement here, *ELSEIF*. It's a combination of *ELSE* and *IF* but without opening another nesting block, so the whole combined block is finished by only one *END IF*.

We only drew the player going to the right in our graphic data, but the Intellivision hardware allows a sprite to be mirorred in the X direction. So to reverse the sprite horizontally, we set a bit in the *SPRITE* using the constant *MIRROR_X* (set to *$0400*).

Also when moving left and right, we make sure the player object is over a girder (modulo 16 equals zero), and then the game extracts the number of the platform to check how far the player can go left (*player_x = player_x - 1*) or right (*player_x = player_x + 1*).

Finally, using *FRAME AND 3* (equivalent to *FRAME* modulo *4*), we check if it's time to switch the animation frames for the player object.

We need some extra code before the *level1_cards:* label:

```
    '
    ' Get vertical offset for sprite
    ' x = Horizontal coordinate
    ' y = Vertical coordinate
    ' returns: offset_y = vertical adjustment in pixels.
    '
get_offset:    PROCEDURE
    position = (y / 8) * 20 + ((x + 4) / 8)
    #c = #backtab(position + 20)
    IF #c = GA THEN offset_y = 0: RETURN
    IF #c = GB THEN offset_y = 1: RETURN
    IF #c = GC THEN offset_y = 2: RETURN
    IF #c = GD THEN offset_y = 3: RETURN
    IF #c = GE THEN offset_y = 4: RETURN
    offset_y = 0
    END


    '
    ' Table for converting disc direction to 4-way direction
    '
controller_direction:
    DATA 0,3,2,3,1,0,2,0
    DATA 4,4,0,0,1,0,0,0
    DATA 0,3,2,0,0,0,0,0
    DATA 4,0,0,0,1,0,0,0
```

The statement *RETURN* means to return from the procedure without executing the rest of the code in the block. *RETURN* can only be used inside a *PROCEDURE*.

Internally, the player object's behavior works like the floors are horizontal, but the procedure *get_offset* adjusts the vertical position of a sprite to stand correctly over the girder. It reads the screen card into *#c* to check what type of girder is the player standing over (*position + 20*).

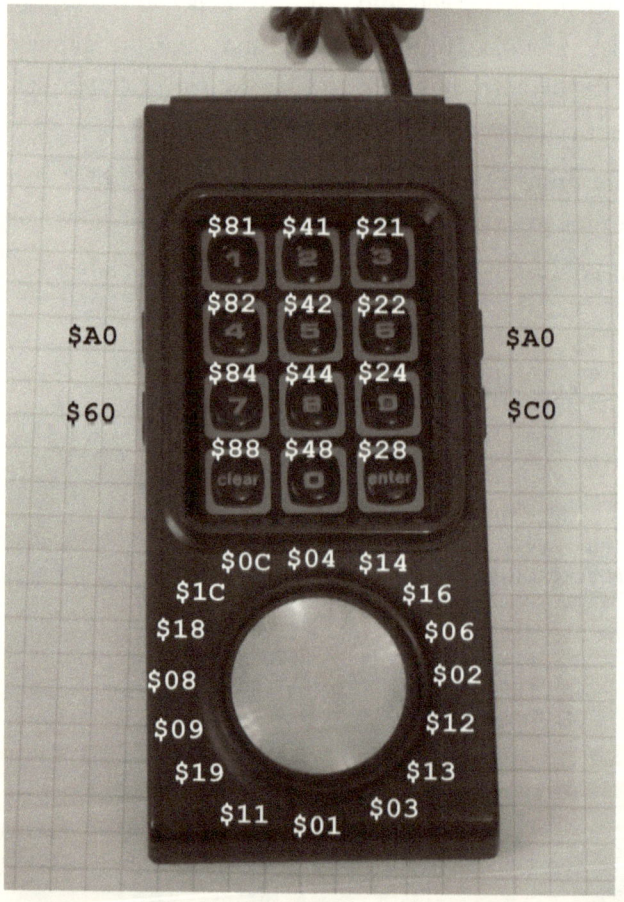

The array *controller_direction* contains a mapping from values 0-31 (the directions provided by the Intellivision controller) to a 4-way direction scheme, using values 1 as up, 2 as right, 3 as down and 4 as left.

Refer to the picture on the previous page to see. For example, how index 4 of controller (up) is mapped to value 1, index 2 (right) is mapped to value 2, index 1 (down) is mapped to value 3, and index 8 (left) is mapped to value 4. The pseudo-diagonals are also mapped in case the player doesn't press the cardinal directions on the disc perfectly, and this makes movement pretty smooth.

Some extra data is required before the *game_bitmaps_0:* label:

```
min_platform:
    DATA 0
    DATA 28
    DATA 20
    DATA 28
    DATA 20
    DATA 12

max_platform:
    DATA 0
    DATA 96
    DATA 123
    DATA 131
    DATA 131
    DATA 139
```

This table indicates the minimum and maximum X coordinate for the player object over each floor.

Now the player can move left and right on the bottom-most platform.

## 5.5 Ladders

The game would be pointless if the player could not go up and down the ladders as there wouldn't be a way to progress.

This code is to be inserted after *d = controller_direction(c AND $1F)*:

```
IF d = 1 THEN ' Going up
    IF player_y % 16 = 0 THEN    ' Over floor
        x = (player_x + 4) / 8
        y = player_y / 8
        IF #backtab(y * 20 + x) = LA THEN
```

```
                    player_y = player_y - 1
                    player_state = 2
              END IF
        ELSEIF (FRAME AND 1) = 0 THEN    ' Over ladder
              player_y = player_y - 1
              IF (FRAME AND 3) = 0 THEN
                    player_state = player_state XOR 4
              END IF
              IF player_y % 16 = 4 THEN
                    player_y = player_y - 4
                    player_state = 0
              END IF
        END IF
     END IF
END IF
IF d = 3 THEN ' Going down
     IF player_y % 16 = 0 THEN      ' Over floor
           x = (player_x + 4) / 8
           y = player_y / 8 + 2
           IF #backtab(y * 20 + x) = LA THEN
                 player_y = player_y + 5
                 player_state = 2
           END IF
     ELSEIF (FRAME AND 1) = 0 THEN      ' Over ladder
           player_y = player_y + 1
           IF (FRAME AND 3) = 0 THEN
                 player_state = player_state XOR 4
           END IF
     END IF
END IF
```

The code above works by checking the current Y coordinate of the player. If it's aligned over a floor, then it checks if there is a ladder under the player (reading the *#backtab* array which is really a direct access to the memory screen) and with the player allowed pixel deviations.

It's moved up (*player_x = player_x - 1*) or down (*player_y = player_y + 1*). The player animation frame is also updated to 2 (in *player_state*)

Going up and down over a ladder makes the player slower by means of *FRAME AND 1* which is equivalent to *FRAME % 2* (FRAME modulo 2 in mathematics). So it moves only one frame every two frames.

To animate the player when going up/down, the *player_state* changes between 2 and 6 (using *XOR 4*) each four video frames (*FRAME AND 3* equivalent to *FRAME % 4*)

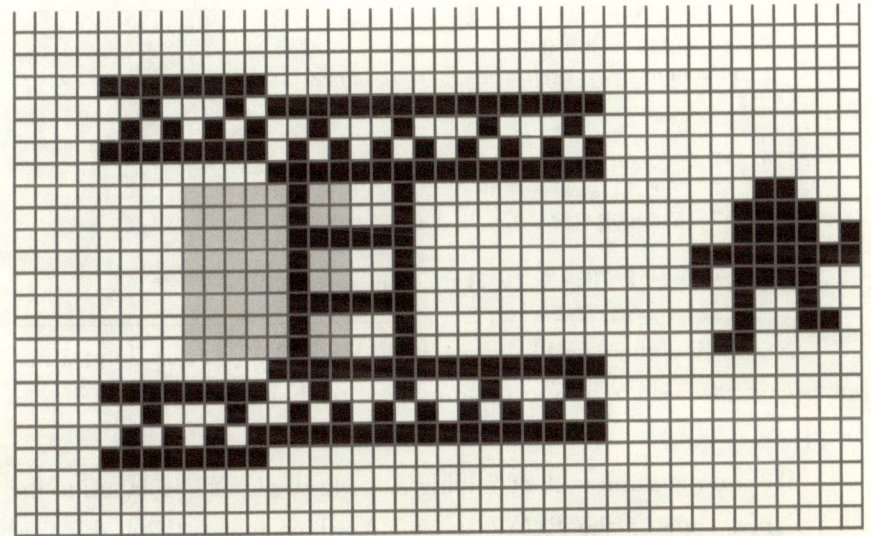

The grey square shows the valid positions for using the ladder.

Compile and run the program, and you'll see how nice it looks!

## 5.6 This game can be won

Let us add the code for the player to move on to the next level. Currently, when the player reaches the top of the screen, it simply stays there without any triggered effect.

Add this before the *restart_level:* label:

```
    #score = 0
    level = 0
    lives = 2

next_level:
    level = level + 1
    IF level > 5 THEN #bonus = 50 ELSE #bonus = 110 - level * 10
```

The code above increases the level number and also generates a bonus score for it.

Now, add the following code just after the *WAIT* in the *game_loop*.

```
IF FRAME % 256 = 0 THEN
    IF #bonus > 0 THEN #bonus = #bonus - 10
END IF

PRINT AT 0 COLOR 7,<5>#score,"0"
PRINT AT 12,<.2>level
PRINT AT 16 COLOR 7,<3>#bonus,"0"

IF player_y = 0 THEN GOTO level_won
```

Notice how the variable *#bonus* is decreased by 10 every 256 frames, but because we add a zero to the display, it really looks like 100 points to the player.

We use the same trick of adding zeros to display *#score* by using the <5> format code of the *PRINT* statement, which means filling this field with zeros to always get 5 digits. Notice that if we use <.5> instead of <5>, the field will be padded with spaces instead of zeros.

The condition to test if the level is completed is simply checking if *player_y* equals zero.

Finally, we insert this code after the line reading *GOTO game_loop*:

```
level_won:
    #score = #score + #bonus
    PRINT AT 0 COLOR 7,<5>#score,"0"
    FOR c = 1 TO 6
        SPRITE c, 0
    NEXT c
    sound_effect = 4: sound_state = 0
    FOR c = 0 TO 60
        WAIT
    NEXT c
    GOTO next_level
```

This code adds the remaining bonus to the score, then waits for a moment before going to the next level.

Run the game, and guide the astronaut to the top and see how the game shows the score, bonus, level number and also how it goes to the next level.

## 5.7 Throw some lunar rocks

It's time for the monkey to throw some lunar rocks at the player. We've used two sprites of the eight available sprites so far, one for the player and another for the monkey's face. So this leaves us with 6 free sprites.

We could program each rock individually but that would cause the source code to grow very large. Instead, we use something new: **arrays**.

Arrays are like using a single piece of land to have a horizontal lot of condominiums and all these condos have the same address (name) but a different number (index).

Insert the following code at the top of the source code before the first *CONST* statement:

```
UNSIGNED #score, #bonus
SIGNED offset_y

DIM rock_x(6)
DIM rock_y(6)
DIM rock_s(6)
```

Notice how it **declares** the arrays to contain rock data. *rock_x* contains the X coordinate of each rock, *rock_y* contains the Y coordinate of each rock and *rock_s* contains each rock state (more on this later).

Each array is indexed from zero to (limit - 1). This means we can access rocks from 0 to 5, but not 6. This is different to **MS-BASIC**.

Before *game_loop:* add this code to set up the rocks.

```
FOR c = 0 TO 5
    rock_y(c) = 0
NEXT c

rock_time = RAND(30) + 10
```

Each rock with (*rock_y* = 0) means that it's not active. While *rock_time* marks the time to add another rock in the frames in a pseudorandom fashion, this time we use *RAND*, which is similar to *RANDOM* except it holds the same value until a video frame passes. This makes *RAND* slightly faster than *RANDOM* but otherwise the syntax is identical. Notice that the *FOR* loop goes to the very limit of the arrays.

We now need a way to display rocks on the screen. Insert this code just after *game_loop:* label:

```
    FOR c = 0 TO 5
        IF rock_y(c) THEN
            x = rock_x(c)
            y = rock_y(c)
            IF rock_s(c) < 2 THEN
                GOSUB get_offset
                IF x = player_x AND y = player_y THEN #score =
#score + 10
            ELSE
                offset_y = 0
            END IF
            SPRITE c + 1, MOB_LEFT + rock_x(c), MOB_TOP +
rock_y(c) + offset_y + rock_mirror((FRAME / 4) AND 3),
rock_animation((FRAME / 4) AND 1)
        ELSE
            SPRITE c + 1, 0
        END IF
    NEXT c
```

The above code processes the data of each rock. If *rock_y(c)* isn't zero, then it uses the X and Y coordinates. It checks the state to see if it's a falling rock (*rock_s* is 2 or 3) and adjusts to floor below the rock.

Notice how it uses *FRAME* divided by 4 (so the animation frame is changed every 4 frames) and ANDed with 3 (equivalent to modulo 4) to animate the rock. You could have used (FRAME / 4) % 4 or (FRAME / 4) AND 3 for same result, it's a matter of taste. The resulting number is between 0 and 3, which is used to select data from the *rock_mirror* and *rock_animation* arrays.

We add some necessary data before the *game_bitmaps_0:* label:

```
rock_animation:
    DATA RA
    DATA RB

rock_mirror:
```

```
DATA $0000
DATA $0000
DATA MIRROR_Y
DATA MIRROR_Y
```

And finally, we need to add the code to manage the rocks (adding a new one and moving existing ones). This code must be inserted after the line with *GOTO level_won*

```
rock_time = rock_time - 1
IF rock_time = 0 THEN
    IF level > 10 THEN c = 60 ELSE c = 60 + 5 * (10 - level)
    rock_time = c + RANDOM(45)
    FOR c = 0 TO 5
        IF rock_y(c) = 0 THEN
            rock_x(c) = 96
            rock_y(c) = 16
            rock_s(c) = 0
            EXIT FOR
        END IF
    NEXT c
END IF

FOR c = 0 TO 5
    IF rock_y(c) THEN
        IF rock_s(c) = 0 THEN
            platform = rock_y(c) / 16
            IF rock_x(c) > min_platform(platform) THEN
                rock_x(c) = rock_x(c) - 1
            ELSE
                rock_y(c) = rock_y(c) + 4
                rock_x(c) = rock_x(c) - 4
                rock_s(c) = 3
            END IF
        ELSEIF rock_s(c) = 1 THEN
            platform = rock_y(c) / 16
            IF rock_x(c) < max_platform(platform) THEN
                rock_x(c) = rock_x(c) + 1
            ELSE
                rock_y(c) = rock_y(c) + 4
                rock_x(c) = rock_x(c) + 4
                rock_s(c) = 2
            END IF
        ELSEIF rock_s(c) >= 2 THEN
            rock_y(c) = rock_y(c) + 1
            IF rock_y(c) >= 96 THEN
```

```
                    rock_y(c) = 0
            ELSEIF rock_y(c) % 16 = 0 THEN
                    rock_s(c) = rock_s(c) % 2
            END IF
        END IF
    END IF
NEXT c
```

The first thing we do is decrement the content of the variable *rock_time* until it's 0, then based on the current level a new *rock_time* is selected for the next rock. It searches the array *rock_y* looking for a value of zero, stating it's a free slot. Once it finds a empty slot, it spawns a rock just left of the monkey at the top platform, the state is set to 0 meaning "go to the left".

The second loop runs over the active rocks and checks in *rock_s* for the state. If it finds a zero then it moves the rock to the left, until it finds the end of girder and changes the rock's state to 3.

If it finds 1 as state, then it moves the rock to the right, until it finds the end of girder and changes the rock's state to 2.

Finally, if the state is greater or equal to 2, then the rock falls vertically (Y coordinate is increased), and if the rock exceeds the screen limits then the rock disappears (marking *rock_y(c) = 0*). Otherwise, if a rock touches the platform directly under it, the state is reassigned modulo 2; thus, state 2 becomes 0 and state 3 becomes 1, changing the direction of the horizontal movement.

## 5.8 Player dies

The player is currently unaffected by rocks but this is about to change. Add this line before *IF player_y = 0 THEN GOTO level_won*

```
IF COL0 AND $007e THEN GOTO player_defeat
```

The special *COL0* variable of IntyBASIC is used here. *COL0* translates to "collisions for sprite 0", and the *AND* value specifies the other sprites with which we want to check collision. In this case, we want sprite number 1 through 6, which is represented by bits 1 through 6, so the value is therefore *$007e*.

After the line *GOTO next_level*, insert this code:

```
player_defeat:
    sound_effect = 3: sound_state = 0
    FOR c = 0 TO 60
        WAIT
        d = (FRAME / 4) AND 3
        IF d = 0 THEN
            SPRITE 0,MOB_LEFT + player_x, MOB_TOP + player_y +
offset_y, PA
        ELSEIF d = 1 THEN
            SPRITE 0,MOB_LEFT + player_x, MOB_TOP + player_y +
offset_y, PD
        ELSEIF d = 2 THEN
            SPRITE 0,MOB_LEFT + player_x, MOB_TOP + MIRROR_X +
MIRROR_Y + player_y + offset_y, PA
        ELSE
            SPRITE 0,MOB_LEFT + player_x, MOB_TOP + MIRROR_X +
MIRROR_Y + player_y + offset_y, PD
        END IF
    NEXT c

    IF lives <> 0 THEN
        lives = lives - 1
        GOTO restart_level
    END IF

    FOR c = 0 TO 6
        SPRITE c, 0
    NEXT c

    PRINT AT 125 COLOR 6,"GAME  OVER"
    FOR c = 0 TO 60
        WAIT
    NEXT c

    DO
        c = CONT
    LOOP WHILE c

    DO
```

```
        c = CONT
LOOP WHILE c = 0

GOTO start_game
```

This code does a 60 frames cycle with the player sprites to make it look like the astronaut is spinning using the sprite mirroring capabilities of the hardware. The game then checks the number of lives remaining. If it isn't zero then it restarts the level, otherwise the program deletes all sprites, shows the GAME OVER message and waits a short time before jumping to start_game.

# 5.9 Jumping

Now we have a problem, the player cannot avoid the rocks! He can go up ladders and try to avoid rocks this way, but it's hard.

We need to add the possibility of jumping.

After the first *player_state = 0* line we need to add this:

```
player_jumping = 0
```

Now we need to replace the code for the player offset, just before *IF player_state = 0 THEN*:

```
IF player_jumping THEN
        offset_y = jump_y(player_jumping - 1) + player_offset
ELSEIF player_state <> 2 AND player_state <> 6 THEN
        GOSUB get_offset
        player_offset = offset_y
ELSE
        offset_y = 0
        player_offset = 0
END IF
```

Add the following code to manage the jumping counter just before *rock_time = rock_time - 1*

```
IF player_jumping THEN
    IF player_jumping = 24 THEN
        player_jumping = 0
    ELSE
        player_jumping = player_jumping + 1
    END IF
END IF
```

We also need to process the side buttons to allow for jumping, replacing the non-working block of code *ELSEIF (d = $60)*:

```
ELSEIF (d = $60) + (d = $a0) + (d = $c0) THEN   ' Side button
    IF player_jumping = 0 THEN
        player_jumping = 1
        sound_effect = 2: sound_state = 0
    END IF
ELSE
```

And finally, we define the jumping offsets so the jump can be smooth and elegant.

Insert the following before *game_bitmaps_0:* label

```
jump_y:
    DATA -2
    DATA -4
    DATA -5
    DATA -6
    DATA -7
    DATA -8
    DATA -9
    DATA -9
    DATA -10
    DATA -10
    DATA -11
    DATA -11
    DATA -11
    DATA -11
    DATA -10
    DATA -10
    DATA -9
    DATA -9
    DATA -8
```

```
DATA -7
DATA -6
DATA -5
DATA -4
DATA -2
```

Now the game is essentially complete. The player can jump over lunar rocks, and can win the game, he can also be defeated. Scoring and bonuses are managed as well.

And of course the game is silent because we're in space, but that's not very interesting, is it?

# 5.10 Sound and final details

If you observed carefully, we've been building the code with references to *sound_effect* and *sound_state*, but no routine uses these variables.

It's time to add a new feature of IntyBASIC at the start of the game:

```
ON FRAME GOSUB play_effects
```

This statement indicates to IntyBASIC to call the subroutine *play_effects* upon every video frame. This subroutine needs to be fast, otherwise it may slow down our game.

The subroutine *play_effects* will play our sound effects while the game is running.

This is the code to play the sound effects and we will add it at the end of the source code for the game.

```
'
' Play sound effects
'
play_effects: PROCEDURE
    ON sound_effect GOSUB sound_none, sound_walk, sound_jump,
sound_death, sound_victory
    END
```

```
sound_none:    PROCEDURE
    SOUND 0,,0
    END

sound_walk:    PROCEDURE
    IF (FRAME AND 15) < 2 THEN SOUND 0,200,10 ELSE SOUND 0,,0
    sound_state = sound_state + 1
    IF sound_state = 3 THEN sound_effect = 0
    END

sound_jump:    PROCEDURE
    SOUND 0,200 - sound_state * 10,10
    sound_state = sound_state + 1
    IF sound_state = 10 THEN sound_effect = 0
    END

sound_death:   PROCEDURE
    SOUND 0,1000 + (sound_state / 4 % 2) * 500,10
    sound_state = sound_state + 1
    IF sound_state = 30 THEN sound_effect = 0
    END

sound_victory:    PROCEDURE
    SOUND 0,150 - sound_state * 5,10
    sound_state = sound_state + 1
    IF sound_state = 10 THEN sound_effect = 0
    END
```

Notice the usage of *ON sound_effect GOSUB*, which means to use the variable *sound_effect* as an index into the labels table. The first one is for the zero value, the second one is for the value 1 and so on (it's like a *switch/case* in C language).

Important: Anything called with *GOSUB* should be marked as *PROCEDURE* otherwise IntyBASIC will generate a program that fails miserably.

And finally to complete the game, we'll add a title screen just after the label *start_game:*

```
CLS
PRINT AT 46 COLOR 7,"Monkey"
PRINT AT 70,"Moon"
```

```
PRINT AT 129,MA,MC
PRINT AT 149,MB,MD
SPRITE 7,MOB_LEFT + 9 * 8 + 4,MOB_TOP + 6 * 8, MF

PRINT AT 202 COLOR 6,"Press any button"

DO
    WAIT
    c = CONT
LOOP WHILE c

DO
    WAIT
    c = CONT
LOOP WHILE c = 0
```

Notice the use of *SPRITE* because we use the monkey graphics on the title screen and we need to add the face color.

Congratulations! Now you have an arcade-like game!

What more can you add? An animated monkey? Another level? More enemies? Add snow to the level for Rev?[1]

---

[1] Actually there is a Rev user in Atariage that always puts snow in each game he releases for Intellivision consoles. This feature has become a running joke for any game announced on the Intellivision forums.

# Chapter 6

## Space Raider

No game development would be complete without a space game with the mandatory deep and compelling back story.

You're a rookie commander, and you've heard there are alien invaders in the Delta quadrant in your galaxy, and since you're looking for a promotion you go to the sector ready to kill as many alien ships as possible.

The game plan is to have a player spaceship at the bottom of the screen and enemies coming from the top of the screen in different configurations.

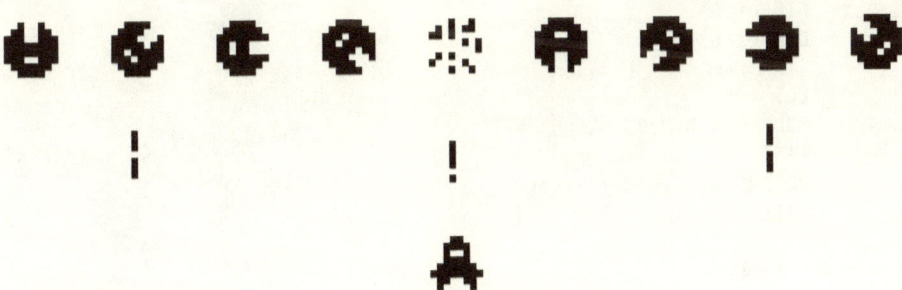

Both the player and enemies can shoot.

Each enemy spaceship can rotate on itself, although we will only use 180 degrees.

As in the other games, we'll start by defining the graphics needed:

```
    '
    ' Space Raider
    ' by Oscar Toledo G.
    ' Creation date: Jun/11/2018.
    '

    UNSIGNED #score

    CONST STAR          = $000E * 8 + 2
    CONST SPRITE_PLAYER    = $0807 + 0 * 8
    CONST SPRITE_SHOT1 = $0805 + 1 * 8
    CONST SPRITE_SHOT2 = $1805 + 2 * 8
    CONST SPRITE_EXPLOSION = $1800 + 3 * 8
    CONST SPRITE_SHIP_1    = $0805 + 4 * 8
    CONST SPRITE_SHIP_2    = $0805 + 5 * 8
    CONST SPRITE_SHIP_3    = $0805 + 6 * 8
    CONST SPRITE_SHIP_4    = $0805 + 7 * 8
    CONST SPRITE_SHIP_5    = $0805 + 8 * 8
    CONST SPRITE_SHIP_6    = $0805 + 9 * 8
    CONST SPRITE_SHIP_7    = $0805 + 10 * 8
    CONST SPRITE_SHIP_8    = $0805 + 11 * 8

    CONST MOB_LEFT     = $0300
    CONSl MOB_TOP      = $0100

    DIM stars(20)

    DIM ex(6)
    DIM ey(6)
    DIM ef(6)
    DIM es(6)

    CLS
    MODE 0,0,0,0,0
    WAIT
    DEFINE 0,12,game_bitmaps
    WAIT
start_game:
    WHILE 1: WEND

    '
    ' Bitmaps used for game
    '
game_bitmaps:
    BITMAP "...XX..."
```

```
BITMAP "..XXXX.."
BITMAP "..X..X.."
BITMAP "..XXXX.."
BITMAP ".XXXXXX."
BITMAP "XXXXXXX"
BITMAP ".XX..XX."
BITMAP ".X....X."

BITMAP "........"
BITMAP "........"
BITMAP "...X...."
BITMAP "...X...."
BITMAP "...X...."
BITMAP "...X...."
BITMAP "........"
BITMAP "...X...."

BITMAP "...X...."
BITMAP "...X...."
BITMAP "...X...."
BITMAP "........"
BITMAP "...X...."
BITMAP "...X...."
BITMAP "...X...."
BITMAP "........"

BITMAP "...X..X."
BITMAP ".X.X.XX."
BITMAP "XX.X...."
BITMAP ".....X.X"
BITMAP ".......X"
BITMAP ".X.X...."
BITMAP "X....X.."
BITMAP "...X..X."

BITMAP "..X..X.."
BITMAP ".XX..XX."
BITMAP "XXX..XXX"
BITMAP "XXXXXXX"
BITMAP "XXXXXXX"
BITMAP "XXX..XXX"
BITMAP ".XXXXXX."
BITMAP "..XXXX.."

BITMAP "..XXXX.."
BITMAP ".XXXX..."
BITMAP "XXXX...X"
BITMAP "XXXXX.XX"
```

```
BITMAP "XX.XXXXX"
BITMAP "XXX.XXXX"
BITMAP ".XXXXXX."
BITMAP "..XXXX.."

BITMAP "..XXXX.."
BITMAP ".XXXXXX."
BITMAP "XXXXXXXX"
BITMAP "XX.XX..."
BITMAP "XX.XX..."
BITMAP "XXXXXXXX"
BITMAP ".XXXXXX."
BITMAP "..XXXX.."

BITMAP "..XXXX.."
BITMAP ".XXXXXX."
BITMAP "XXX.XXXX"
BITMAP "XX.XXXXX"
BITMAP "XXXXX.XX"
BITMAP "XXXX...X"
BITMAP ".XXXX..."
BITMAP "..XXXX.."

BITMAP "..XXXX.."
BITMAP ".XXXXXX."
BITMAP "XXX..XXX"
BITMAP "XXXXXXXX"
BITMAP "XXXXXXXX"
BITMAP "XXX..XXX"
BITMAP ".XX..XX."
BITMAP "..X..X.."

BITMAP "..XXXX.."
BITMAP ".XXXXXX."
BITMAP "XXXX.XXX"
BITMAP "XXXXX.XX"
BITMAP "XX.XXXXX"
BITMAP "X...XXXX"
BITMAP "...XXXX."
BITMAP "..XXXX.."

BITMAP "..XXXX.."
BITMAP ".XXXXXX."
BITMAP "XXXXXXXX"
BITMAP "...XX.XX"
BITMAP "...XX.XX"
BITMAP "XXXXXXXX"
BITMAP ".XXXXXX."
```

```
BITMAP "..XXXX.."

BITMAP "..XXXX.."
BITMAP "...XXXX."
BITMAP "X...XXXX"
BITMAP "XX.XXXXX"
BITMAP "XXXXX.XX"
BITMAP "XXXX.XXX"
BITMAP ".XXXXXX."
BITMAP "..XXXX.."
```

Nothing new this time around except for the pre-declaration of the arrays needed for a background of stars and for the enemies and the projectiles.

# 6.1 A stars background

Let us add a background of stars, replacing the *WHILE 1: WEND*

```
CLS

FOR c = 0 TO 19
    stars(c) = (RANDOM(11) + 1) * 20 + c
    #backtab(stars(c)) = STAR
NEXT c


'
' Main game loop
'
game_loop:
    '
    ' Synchronize game
    '
    WAIT


    '
    ' Move stars backdrop
    '
    c = FRAME AND 1
    start = c * 10
    last = start + 9
    FOR c = start TO last
        d = stars(c)
        #backtab(d) = 0
        IF d >= 220 THEN d = d - 200 ELSE d = d + 20
```

```
        #backtab(d) = STAR
        stars(c) = d
NEXT c

GOTO game_loop
```

The first part of the code puts stars on the screen (technically the star is simply a period character taken from the Intellivision GROM), for each column we put a star on a random line of the screen, except for the first line, which is the reason for *RANDOM(11) + 1*. The multiplication by 20, is to put it on the desired line plus the value of *c* for the desired column.

Inside the game loop, there's a *WAIT* to synchronize with the video chips' refresh rate, and avoid a tearing effect when moving the stars. The next step is to update 10 stars. The stars being updated are chosen by the video frame number, on even frames the stars 0 to 9 are updated, and on odd frames the stars 10 to 19 are updated.

The program takes the current position contained in *stars(c)* and saves it in *d* for faster processing. Then it erases the star from the screen (*#backtab(d) = 0*), and then if the star hasn't reached the bottom of the screen, then it is moved down one row, otherwise it jumps back to the top of the screen, on the second row. (*#backtab(d) = STAR*)

At the end of the *FOR* loop, the new position is saved in *stars(c)*.

This algorithm has a problem. The initial star pattern repeats endlessly. So let us add some randomization to the starting row of each star. Replace the line *IF d >= 220* with this:

```
    IF d >= 220 THEN    ' Star exiting
        IF RANDOM(2) THEN
            d = d - 180    ' Start in 3rd row.
        ELSE
            d = d - 200    ' Start in 2nd row.
        END IF
    ELSE
        d = d + 20    ' Go to next row
    END IF
```

## 6.2 A player and his bullet

Like in our previous game, the next step is to display the player's ship. We start by initializing variables relative to the player's position. These variables are *player_x* and *player_y*, and we also have a variable *crash* to indicate the explosion of the player. There's also *shot_x* and *shot_y* for the bullet position, plus *shot_exp* for indicating the explosion of the bullet.

This code replaces *game_loop*:

```
    '
    ' Restart game after losing live
    '
restart_game:
    player_x = 84
    player_y = 88
    shot_y = 0
    '
    ' Main game loop
    '
game_loop:
    IF crash THEN
        SPRITE 0, MOB_LEFT + player_x, MOB_TOP + player_y,
SPRITE_EXPLOSION + (RAND % 8)
    ELSE
        SPRITE 0, MOB_LEFT + player_x, MOB_TOP + player_y,
SPRITE_PLAYER
    END IF
    IF shot_y = 0 THEN
        SPRITE 1, 0
    ELSEIF shot_exp <> 0 THEN
        SPRITE 1, MOB_LEFT + shot_x, MOB_TOP + shot_y,
SPRITE_EXPLOSION
    ELSE
        SPRITE 1, MOB_LEFT + shot_x, MOB_TOP + shot_y, SPRITE_SHOT1
    END IF
```

As you can see, the code displays the player using *SPRITE 0* and the bullet using *SPRITE 1*.

The following code goes before *GOTO game_loop*.

```
    '
    ' Move player shot
    '
```

71

```
IF shot_y <> 0 THEN
    IF shot_exp THEN
        shot_exp = shot_exp - 1
        IF shot_exp = 0 THEN shot_y = 0
    ELSE
        IF shot_y > 2 THEN
            shot_y = shot_y - 3
        ELSE
            shot_y = 0
        END IF
    END IF
END IF


' Allow player movement
'
c = CONT
d = c AND $E0
IF (d = $80) + (d = $40) + (d = $20) THEN
    ' Keypad pressed
ELSE
    IF (d = $60) + (d = $a0) + (d = $c0) THEN  ' Side button
        IF shot_y = 0 THEN
            shot_x = player_x
            shot_y = player_y
            shot_exp = 0
        END IF
    END IF
    d = controller_direction(c AND $1F)
    IF d = 2 THEN
        IF player_x < 160 THEN player_x = player_x + 2
    END IF
    IF d = 4 THEN
        IF player_x > 8 THEN player_x = player_x - 2
    END IF
END IF
```

The code reads the controllers and moves the spaceship left and right in 2-pixel increments on each frame, detecting the limits of the screen. A bullet is fired if any of the side buttons are pressed.

We shouldn't forget to add the *controller_direction* table just after *GOTO game_loop*

```
controller_direction:
    DATA 0,3,2,3,1,0,2,0
    DATA 4,4,0,0,1,0,0,0
    DATA 0,3,2,0,0,0,0,0
    DATA 4,0,0,0,1,0,0,0
```

# 6.3 Enemies everywhere

Our space backdrop is pretty empty without some enemies. The enemies will be coming in waves. Only 3 ships at the same time, but interesting enough for our purposes.

We already defined the *ex*, *ey*, *ef* and *es* arrays earlier in this chapter. These will respectively contain the X coordinate, Y coordinate, frame number, and state of each enemy ship.

Insert this code before the line saying *restart_game:*

```
#score = 0
lives = 2

FOR c = 0 TO 5
    ex(c) = 0
NEXT c

next_wave = 100 + RANDOM(40)
```

Just before the *WAIT* with the comment "Synchronize the game", insert this code:

```
something = 0
FOR c = 0 TO 2
    IF ex(c) THEN
        SPRITE 2 + c, MOB_LEFT + ex(c), MOB_TOP + (ey(c) AND
$7F), sprite_frame(ef(c))
        something = 1
    ELSE
        SPRITE 2 + c, 0
    END IF
NEXT c
FOR c = 3 TO 5
    IF ex(c) THEN
```

```
            SPRITE 2 + c, MOB_LEFT + ex(c), MOB_TOP + (ey(c) AND
$7F), sprite_frame(9)
                something = 1
        ELSE
                SPRITE 2 + c, 0
        END IF
    NEXT c
```

This code will use the extra sprites to display the enemies if these are valid (*ex(c) = 0* means an inactive enemy). The enemy frame *ef(c)* is passed through a table.

Notice that the variable *something* indicates whether there is still at least one enemy on the screen to prevent another wave.

We need the *sprite_frame* table, so insert this code before the *controller_direction* table:

```
    '
    ' Sprite frames
    '
sprite_frame:
    DATA SPRITE_SHIP_1
    DATA SPRITE_SHIP_2
    DATA SPRITE_SHIP_3
    DATA SPRITE_SHIP_4
    DATA SPRITE_SHIP_5
    DATA SPRITE_SHIP_6
    DATA SPRITE_SHIP_7
    DATA SPRITE_SHIP_8
    DATA SPRITE_EXPLOSION
    DATA SPRITE_SHOT2
```

Now we need to change the time to start an enemy wave. This code goes before the comment "Move player shot":

```
    '
    ' Count time to next wave or move current wave
    '
    IF next_wave THEN
        IF something = 0 THEN
            next_wave = next_wave - 1
        ELSE
```

```
                ON wave GOSUB move_wave_0
        END IF
    ELSE
        next_wave = 20 + RANDOM(20)
        wave = 0 ' Temporary
        ON wave GOSUB start_wave_0_1
    END IF
```

We only have one wave for now, in order to test the concept.

Add the code below (to start and move enemy wave) just after *GOTO*
*game_loop*:

```
    '
    ' Start waves 0 and 1
    '
start_wave_0_1:    PROCEDURE
    c = player_x
    IF c < 24 THEN c = 24
    IF c > 144 THEN c = 144
    x = RANDOM(32) + player_x - 16
    ex(0) = x - 16
    ey(0) = -16
    ef(0) = 4
    ex(1) = x
    ey(1) = -8
    ef(1) = 4
    ex(2) = x + 16
    ey(2) = -16
    ef(2) = 4
    wave_state = 0
    END


    '
    ' Move wave 0
    '
move_wave_0: PROCEDURE
    wave_state = wave_state + 1
    IF wave_state = 120 THEN
        ex(0) = 0: ex(1) = 0: ex(2) = 0
        RETURN
    END IF
    IF wave_state >= 32 AND wave_state <= 39 THEN
        IF ex(0) THEN
            ef(0) = 5
            ex(0) = ex(0) - 1
        END IF
```

```
                IF ex(1) THEN
                    ef(1) = 5
                    ex(1) = ex(1) - 1
                END IF
                IF ex(2) THEN
                    ef(2) = 5
                    ex(2) = ex(2) - 1
                END IF
            ELSEIF wave_state = 40 THEN
                ef(0) = 4
                ef(1) = 4
                ef(2) = 4
            ELSEIF wave_state >= 64 AND wave_state <= 71 THEN
                IF ex(0) THEN
                    ef(0) = 3
                    ex(0) = ex(0) + 1
                END IF
                IF ex(1) THEN
                    ef(1) = 3
                    ex(1) = ex(1) + 1
                END IF
                IF ex(2) THEN
                    ef(2) = 3
                    ex(2) = ex(2) + 1
                END IF
            ELSEIF wave_state = 72 THEN
                ef(0) = 4
                ef(1) = 4
                ef(2) = 4
            END IF

            IF ex(0) THEN
                ey(0) = ey(0) + 1
            END IF
            IF ex(1) THEN
                ey(1) = ey(1) + 1
            END IF
            IF ex(2) THEN
                ey(2) = ey(2) + 1
            END IF
            END
```

As a labor of love, the *start_wave_0_1* procedure bases the X
coordinate of the trio of ships on the X coordinate of the player's ship, plus
a random number with each spaceship facing down.

Configuration of enemies for wave 0 and 1

Then the *move_wave_0* procedure moves the spaceships in a downwards direction, increasing the variable *wave_state*. Once this variable reaches a certain value, it moves the ships to the left and to the right. It also changes the graphic frame of the enemy spaceships to give the illusion that the ships are turning.

## 6.4 Battle in space

Even though the spaceships are moving and the player can shoot them down them, there is no collision detection.

But we don't want to shoot peaceful ships, so let's give the enemies the ability to shoot at the player by inserting this code before the comment "Move player shot":

```
'
' Create and move enemy bullets
'
FOR c = 3 TO 5
    IF ex(c) THEN
        ey(c) = ey(c) + 2
        IF ey(c) >= 104 THEN ex(c) = 0
```

```
        ELSEIF ex(c - 3) THEN
            IF RANDOM(2) THEN
                ex(c) = ex(c - 3)
                ey(c) = ey(c - 3)
            END IF
        END IF
    NEXT c
```

And now, add this code before the comment "Move stars backdrop":

```
    '
    ' Check for collision between player's ship and enemies or
bullets
    '
    IF COL0 AND $00FC THEN
        IF crash = 0 THEN crash = 60
    END IF

    '
    ' Check collision of player bullet against enemies
    '
    IF COL1 AND $00FC THEN
        c = 255
        IF COL2 AND $0002 THEN c = 0
        IF COL3 AND $0002 THEN c = 1
        IF COL4 AND $0002 THEN c = 2
        IF COL5 AND $0002 THEN c = 3
        IF COL6 AND $0002 THEN c = 4
        IF COL7 AND $0002 THEN c = 5
        IF c < 3 THEN ' Handle enemy destroyed
            IF ex(c) THEN
                shot_x = ex(c)
                shot_y = ey(c)
                shot_exp = 4
                ex(c) = 0
                #score = #score + 1
            END IF
        ELSEIF c < 6 THEN  ' Handle destruction of bullet
            ex(c) = 0
        END IF
    END IF
```

And then insert this code before the "Count time to next wave or move current wave" comment:

```
'
' Update score and number of lives
'
PRINT AT 0 COLOR 3,<5>#score,"0"
#backtab(19) = (lives + $10) * 8 + 3


'
' Count time of crash to go to game over
'
IF crash THEN
    crash = crash - 1
    IF crash = 0 THEN GOTO game_over
END IF
```

Finally, add this after *GOTO game_loop*

```
'
' Game over
'
game_over:
    FOR c = 0 TO 7
        SPRITE c, 0
    NEXT c

    IF lives <> 0 THEN
        lives = lives - 1
        GOTO restart_game
    END IF

    PRINT AT 85 COLOR 6,"GAME  OVER"

    FOR c = 0 TO 60
        WAIT
    NEXT c

    DO
        c = CONT
    LOOP WHILE c

    DO
        c = CONT
    LOOP WHILE c = 0

    GOTO start_game
```

And the core of the game is now complete.

# 6.5 More attack waves

The game gets a little monotonous after several minutes, so let us add different attack waves to keep the player engaged.

The first wave group only moves the left-most and right-most enemy ships, the center one doesn't do much.

First, let us alter the code to add the wave:

```
'
' Count time to next wave or move current wave
'
IF next_wave THEN
    IF something = 0 THEN
        next_wave = next_wave - 1
    ELSE
        ON wave GOSUB move_wave_0, move_wave_1
    END IF
ELSE
    next_wave = 20 + RANDOM(20)
    wave = RANDOM(2)
    ON wave GOSUB start_wave_0_1, start_wave_0_1
END IF
```

We are reusing the code for *start_wave_0_1*, and now we add the *move_wave_1* procedure:

```
'
' Move wave 1
'
move_wave_1: PROCEDURE
    wave_state = wave_state + 1
    IF wave_state = 120 THEN
        ex(0) = 0: ex(1) = 0: ex(2) = 0
        RETURN
    END IF
    IF wave_state >= 32 AND wave_state <= 39 THEN
        IF ex(0) THEN
            ef(0) = 5
            ex(0) = ex(0) - 1
        END IF
        IF ex(2) THEN
            ef(2) = 3
            ex(2) = ex(2) + 1
        END IF
```

```
ELSEIF wave_state = 40 THEN
    ef(0) = 4
    ef(2) = 4
ELSEIF wave_state >= 64 AND wave_state <= 71 THEN
    IF ex(0) THEN
        ef(0) = 3
        ex(0) = ex(0) + 1
    END IF
    IF ex(2) THEN
        ef(2) = 5
        ex(2) = ex(2) - 1
    END IF
ELSEIF wave_state = 72 THEN
    ef(0) = 4
    ef(2) = 4
END IF

IF ex(0) THEN
    ey(0) = ey(0) + 1
END IF
IF ex(1) THEN
    ey(1) = ey(1) + 1
END IF
IF ex(2) THEN
    ey(2) = ey(2) + 1
END IF
END
```

Now you can test the new wave.

Let us add wave 2, where only a pair of enemies descend moving quickly left and right.

Configuration of enemy ships for wave 2

In the same manner as the previous wave, we change the calling code.

```
'
' Count time to next wave or move the current wave
'
IF next_wave THEN
    IF something = 0 THEN
        next_wave = next_wave - 1
    ELSE
        ON wave GOSUB move_wave_0, move_wave_1, move_wave_2
    END IF
ELSE
    next_wave = 20 + RANDOM(20)
    wave = RANDOM(2)
    ON wave GOSUB start_wave_0_1, start_wave_0_1, start_wave_2
END IF
```

And now we add the code to start and move the wave.

```
'
' Start wave 2
'
start_wave_2: PROCEDURE
    c = player_x
    IF c < 24 THEN c = 24
    IF c > 144 THEN c = 144
    x = RANDOM(32) + player_x - 16
    ex(0) = x - 8
    ey(0) = -8
    ef(0) = 4
    ex(1) = x + 8
    ey(1) = -8
    ef(1) = 4
    wave_state = 0
    END


    '
    ' Move wave 2
    '
move_wave_2: PROCEDURE
    wave_state = wave_state + 1
    IF wave_state = 120 THEN
        ex(0) = 0: ex(1) = 0: ex(2) = 0
        RETURN
    END IF
    c = wave_state AND 31
    IF c < 12 THEN
```

```
        IF ex(0) THEN
            ex(0) = ex(0) - 1
            ef(0) = 5
        END IF
        IF ex(1) THEN
            ex(1) = ex(1) - 1
            ef(1) = 5
        END IF
    ELSEIF c < 16 THEN
        ef(0) = 4
        ef(1) = 4
    ELSEIF c < 28 THEN
        IF ex(0) THEN
            ex(0) = ex(0) + 1
            ef(0) = 3
        END IF
        IF ex(1) THEN
            ex(1) = ex(1) + 1
            ef(1) = 3
        END IF
    ELSE
        ef(0) = 4
        ef(1) = 4
    END IF

    IF ex(0) THEN
        ey(0) = ey(0) + 1
    END IF
    IF ex(1) THEN
        ey(1) = ey(1) + 1
    END IF
    END
```

This is all somewhat repetitive, so we add a fourth wave where enemies appear from the sides of the screen and then descend together. Again, we alter the calling code:

```
'
' Count time to next wave or move the current wave
'
IF next_wave THEN
    IF something = 0 THEN
        next_wave = next_wave - 1
    ELSE
```

```
                    ON wave GOSUB move_wave_0, move_wave_1, move_wave_2,
move_wave_3
        END IF
    ELSE
        next_wave = 20 + RANDOM(20)
        wave = RANDOM(4)
        ON wave GOSUB start_wave_0_1, start_wave_0_1, start_wave_2,
start_wave_3
    END IF
```

Configuration of enemies for wave 3

And now we add the code for the new attack wave:

```
    '
    ' Start wave 3
    '
start_wave_3: PROCEDURE
    ex(0) = 1
    ey(0) = 16
    ef(0) = 2
    ex(1) = 168
    ey(1) = 16
    ef(1) = 6
    wave_state = 0
    END


    '
    ' Move wave 3
    '
move_wave_3: PROCEDURE
    wave_state = wave_state + 1
    IF wave_state = 184 THEN
        ex(0) = 0: ex(1) = 0: ex(2) = 0
        RETURN
    END IF
```

```
IF wave_state < 72 THEN
    IF ex(0) THEN
        ex(0) = ex(0) + 1
    END IF
    IF ex(1) THEN
        ex(1) = ex(1) - 1
    END IF
ELSEIF wave_state < 80 THEN
    IF ex(0) THEN
        ex(0) = ex(0) + 1
        ey(0) = ey(0) + 1
        ef(0) = 3
    END IF
    IF ex(1) THEN
        ex(1) = ex(1) - 1
        ey(1) = ey(1) + 1
        ef(1) = 5
    END IF
ELSE
    IF ex(0) THEN
        ey(0) = ey(0) + 1
        ef(0) = 4
    END IF
    IF ex(1) THEN
        ey(1) = ey(1) + 1
        ef(1) = 4
    END IF
END IF
END
```

## 6.6 The title screen

We are missing the title screen for this game. After the label *start_game:*
insert this code:

```
CLS
PRINT AT 44 COLOR 7,"Space Raider"

PRINT AT 182 COLOR 6,"Press any button"

DO
    WAIT
    c = CONT
LOOP WHILE c
```

```
DO
     WAIT
     c = CONT
LOOP WHILE c = 0
```

We're also missing sound effects. Can we do something about that?

We need four sound effects, one for when player the shoots, one for when an enemy shoots, one for the explosion of the player's ship and one for the explosion of an enemy ship.

This time we'll make multichannel sound effects, so we can hear the player and the enemy firing their shots at the same time.

Let us add the sound effect for the explosion of the player's ship:

```
IF COL0 AND $00FC THEN
     IF crash = 0 THEN crash = 60: sound_explosion1 = 1
END IF
```

Now for the enemy's explosion:

```
IF ex(c) THEN
     shot_x = ex(c)
     shot_y = ey(c)
     shot_exp = 4
     ex(c) = 0
     #score = #score + 1
     sound_explosion2 = 1
END IF
```

When an enemy fires a new bullet:

```
IF RANDOM(2) THEN
     ex(c) = ex(c - 3)
     ey(c) = ey(c - 3)
     sound_shot2 = 1
END IF
```

And when the player shoots a bullet:

```
            IF shot_y = 0 THEN
                  shot_x = player_x
                  shot_y = player_y
                  shot_exp = 0
                  sound_shot1 = 1
            END IF
```

And now add the following line of code as the first line of source code of the game:

```
ON FRAME GOSUB play_effects
```

Then add this at the very end of the source code:

```
    '
    ' Play sound effects
    '
play_effects: PROCEDURE
    IF sound_explosion1 THEN
        SOUND 0, 2000, 15 - sound_explosion1 / 4
        SOUND 4, sound_explosion1 / 2 + 4,$30
        sound_explosion1 = sound_explosion1 + 1
        IF sound_explosion1 = 50 THEN sound_explosion1 = 0
    ELSEIF sound_explosion2 THEN
        SOUND 0, 1000, 15 - sound_explosion2 / 2
        SOUND 4, sound_explosion2 + 12,$30
        sound_explosion2 = sound_explosion2 + 1
        IF sound_explosion2 = 20 THEN sound_explosion2 = 0
    ELSEIF sound_shot1 THEN
        SOUND 0, 100 - sound_shot1 * 5, 12
        SOUND 4,,$38
        sound_shot1 = sound_shot1 + 1
        IF sound_shot1 = 11 THEN sound_shot1 = 0
    ELSE
        SOUND 0,,0
        SOUND 4,,$38
    END IF
    IF sound_shot2 THEN
        SOUND 1, 50 + sound_shot2 * 7, 12
        sound_shot2 = sound_shot2 + 1
        IF sound_shot2 = 6 THEN sound_shot2 = 0
    ELSE
        SOUND 1,,0
```

```
END IF
END
```

Notice how we are using *SOUND 0* and *SOUND 1* for independent tones.

We're also using the mixer of the AY-3-8914 sound chip to enable noise for explosions. The second argument in *SOUND 4* modifies the noise frequency and the third argument handles the mixer bits. See Appendix B for more information.

# Chapter 7

## Bouncy Cube

Let us make a game where a cube bounces on the screen avoiding obstacles. These type of games are common on mobile platforms. The difference is that we're be making it for the Intellivision, and we're going to be using the hardware scrolling features. Plus we'll be using the IntyColor utility to create a full blown title screen.

So far we have used the minimal capabilities of IntyBASIC, however it includes a utility called IntyColor to convert images in BMP format to a format understandable by the Intellivision.

You can basically use any bitmap editing software to create your images, including MS-Paint, GIMP and even Photoshop®.

The only caveat is to limit yourself to the Intellivision colors. The IntyColor utility tries to approximately convert your colors to match the hardware colors, but you can also use the hardware colors directly.

| Intellivision Colors | Red | Green | Blue |
|---|---|---|---|
| 0 = Black | 0 | 0 | 0 |
| 1 = Red | 0 | 45 | 255 |
| 2 = Blue | 255 | 61 | 16 |
| 3 = Tan | 201 | 207 | 171 |
| 4 = Dark green | 56 | 107 | 63 |

| Intellivision Colors | Red | Green | Blue |
| --- | --- | --- | --- |
| 5 = Green | 0 | 167 | 86 |
| 6 = Yellow | 250 | 234 | 80 |
| 7 = White | 255 | 255 | 255 |
| 8 = Grey | 189 | 172 | 200 |
| 9 = Cyan | 36 | 184 | 255 |
| 10 = Orange | 255 | 180 | 31 |
| 11 = Brown | 84 | 110 | 0 |
| 12 = Pink | 255 | 78 | 87 |
| 13 = Light blue | 164 | 150 | 255 |
| 14 = Yellow green | 117 | 204 | 128 |
| 15 = Purple | 181 | 26 | 88 |

Some of the colors vary wildly on real Intellivision hardware, typically the colors pink and purple, so make sure to test your software on a real console before shipping your game (wink).

In this case the image we'll be processing is this one of 96x56 pixels:

Given the name *bouncy_cube.bmp*, we need to pass it through IntyColor to create the Intellivision screen data. Of course, you should have extracted the IntyColor executable from the IntyBASIC distribution, then you can run it via command line from the folder with the executable. Switch to intycolor_linux if you're using Linux or remove the "./" characters if you're using Windows.

```
./intycolor -b -n bouncy_cube.bmp bouncy_cube.bas title
```

You can run IntyColor without any option or filename in order to see the usage manual. For the purpose of this accelerated tutorial, we'll say that -b means *generate data for IntyBASIC* and -n means *generate only data instead of a runnable program*. The first filename is the image, the second filename is for the IntyBASIC data and the third one is a label for the data.

The generated *bouncy_cube.bas* file looks like this:

```
    REM IntyColor v1.1.5 Jul/25/2017
    REM Command: ./intycolor -b -n bouncy_cube.bmp bouncy_cube.bas
title
    REM Created: Sat Jun 30 21:28:46 2018

    ' 46 bitmaps
title_bitmaps_0:
    DATA $0300,$0303,$0303,$0303
    DATA $F000,$B8F8,$BBB9,$FBE3
    DATA $0000,$0000,$FBF3,$BBBB
    DATA $0000,$0000,$BBBB,$BBBB
    DATA $0000,$0000,$FBB1,$BBBB
    DATA $0000,$0000,$FFF7,$BBBB
    DATA $0000,$0000,$3838,$B030
    DATA $3E00,$777F,$7777,$7070
    DATA $0000,$0000,$7777,$7777
    DATA $7000,$7070,$7F76,$7777
    DATA $0000,$0000,$7F3E,$7F77
    DATA $0303,$0303,$0303,$0000
    DATA $BBBB,$BBBB,$F1FB,$0000
    DATA $BBBB,$BBBB,$BBFB,$0000
    DATA $BBBB,$BBBB,$B9BB,$0000
    DATA $BB83,$B9B9,$E3F1,$0003
title_bitmaps_1:
    DATA $B0B0,$F0B0,$E0F0,$00E0
    DATA $7777,$7777,$3C7E,$0000
    DATA $7777,$7777,$377F,$0000
    DATA $7777,$7777,$767F,$0000
    DATA $707F,$7777,$3E7F,$0000
```

```
     DATA $FFFF,$FCFE,$E0F0,$0080
     DATA $80C1,$2020,$2020,$1010
     DATA $0FFF,$0001,$0000,$0000
     DATA $FFFF,$3FFF,$0003,$0000
     DATA $FFFF,$FFFF,$3FFF,$0F1F
     DATA $0000,$8000,$8080,$8080
     DATA $1010,$1010,$1010,$0810
     DATA $1800,$4224,$8D81,$244E
     DATA $0000,$0403,$0E08,$0306
     DATA $0F0F,$8F0F,$4F4F,$0F8F
     DATA $FFFF,$FFFF,$FFFF,$E0FF
title_bitmaps_2:
     DATA $FFFF,$FFFF,$F0FF,$0000
     DATA $FFFF,$F0FF,$0000,$0000
     DATA $FFFF,$0000,$0000,$0000
     DATA $00FF,$0000,$0000,$0000
     DATA $8080,$C080,$C0C0,$C0C0
     DATA $0808,$0808,$0808,$0808
     DATA $0018,$0C00,$070F,$0003
     DATA $0000,$0C00,$F0F8,$00E0
     DATA $0F0F,$0F0F,$0F0F,$0F0F
     DATA $C0C0,$FFF8,$FFFF,$FFFF
     DATA $0808,$0808,$FFC0,$FFFF
     DATA $0000,$0000,$FF07,$FFFF
     DATA $0000,$0700,$FFFF,$FFFF
     DATA $0F0F,$FF0F,$FFFF,$FFFF


     REM 12x7 cards
title_cards:
     DATA $0802,$080A,$0812,$081A,$0822,$082A,$0832,$083A,
$0842,$084A,$0852,$0000
     DATA $085A,$0862,$0862,$086A,$0872,$087A,$0882,$088A,
$0892,$089A,$08A2,$0000
     DATA
$0000,$0000,$0000,$0000,$0000,$0000,$0000,$0000,$0000,$0000,$0000,$0
000
     DATA
$0000,$0000,$0000,$0000,$0000,$0000,$0000,$1AA8,$1AB0,$1AB8,$1AC0,$1
AC8
     DATA
$2600,$2600,$2600,$2600,$2600,$2600,$2600,$1AD0,$1AD8,$1AE0,$1AE8,$1
AF0
     DATA $08FF,$0907,$090F,$0917,$091F,$091F,
$0000,$1B20,$1B28,$1B30,$1B38,$1B40
     DATA
$0000,$0000,$0000,$0000,$0000,$0000,$0000,$1B48,$1B50,$1B58,$1B60,$1
B68
```

It's an ugly set of bitmaps and STIC cards to display the image but when auto-generated by IntyColor, it saves a **great** deal of time.

This image uses 46x4 words for bitmaps (so 184 words), plus 84 words for the cards. In a small game, this isn't a problem but if the game includes many images then you should take a look at Appendix A, section A.4.

# 7.1 Displaying the title screen

We'll be using a new IntyBASIC statement: INCLUDE, which allows the inclusion of another file inside the main file at compile time.

Let us display the title screen, by inserting this code inside *bouncy.bas*:

```
'
' Bouncy Cube
'
' by Oscar Toledo G.
'
' Creation date: Jun/24/2018.
' Revision date: Jun/30/2018. Completed.
'

    CONST SPEED = 2         ' Scrolling speed
    CONST SMILEY_X = 48     ' X-coordinate of player

    DIM sx(8), sy(8)   ' Player shadow

    PLAY SIMPLE NO DRUMS

    '
    ' Show title screen
    '
title_screen:
    PLAY OFF  ' Turn off sound
    CLS        ' Clears the screen
    MODE 1         ' FGBG screen mode
    SCROLL 0,0,0  ' Reset scroll
    BORDER 0,0     ' Reset border
    FOR c = 0 TO 7' Erase sprites
        SPRITE c, 0
    NEXT c
    WAIT
    DEFINE 0,16,title_bitmaps_0
```

```
WAIT
DEFINE 16,16,title_bitmaps_1
WAIT
DEFINE 32,14,title_bitmaps_2
WAIT

'
' The title screen sizes at 12x7 cards
' Centers it on the screen (card 24)
'
SCREEN title_cards,0,24,12,7,12

PRINT AT 205 COLOR 7,"PRESS DISC"

'
' Wait until disc is pressed
'
count = 0
DO
    WAIT
    IF count < 30 THEN count = count + 1
    c = CONT
LOOP WHILE c = 0 OR c > 31 OR count < 30

WHILE 1: WEND

'
' Our awesome title screen
'
INCLUDE "bouncy_cube.bas"
```

The other new statements in this program are BORDER, SCROLL and the fancy arguments for SCREEN.

BORDER allows us to specify a color for the area surrounding the main graphics screen, and **also** to mask the top row and left column of the screen for scrolling. Check appendix A for the full syntax.

The SCROLL statement lets us define a pixel offset of 0 to 7 pixels for each X and Y coordinates, moving the screen in pixel increments. However, the screen **cannot** move beyond an offset of 7, so the programmer must do some work to shift all cards on the screen by one position (up, down, left or right).

So IntyBASIC comes to the rescue, with the third argument that selects the required displacement (see Appendix A) to be done as soon as the hardware finishes displaying the current video frame, and also does it fast enough to make scrolling games possible. Notice that it uses twenty of the available 16-bit variables and these are scarce on the Intellivision.

## 7.2 The player

We are going to use a rotating cube as the image of the player's avatar. Such eye-candy is completely unneeded for the purposes of the game, but it lets us do something that makes the game pleasant to the eye.

The graphics are all in a file called *smiley.bas* because these are "auto-magically" generated by the program *smiley.c*. This program is not going to be explained but it's simple enough and it's listed in Appendix D.

The player's avatar has 72 frames of animation, each one covers a span of 5 degrees for a total of 360 degrees.

Also, for the first time, we'll be using 8x16 sprites but compressed on the vertical side for higher resolution.

For this book, we wanted to include the "visual" version where you see each sprite, so see below:

```
smiley_bitmaps:
    BITMAP "........"   ' 0 degrees
    BITMAP "........"
    BITMAP "........"
    BITMAP "..XXXXX."
    BITMAP "..X...X."
    BITMAP "..X...X."
    BITMAP "..XX.XX."
    BITMAP "..X...X."
    BITMAP "..X...X."
    BITMAP "..X...X."
    BITMAP "..X...X."
    BITMAP "..X...X."
    BITMAP "..X...X."
    BITMAP "..XXXXX."
    BITMAP "........"
    BITMAP "........"
```

```
        BITMAP "........"  ' 5 degrees
        BITMAP "........"
        BITMAP "........"
        BITMAP "..XXX..."
        BITMAP "..X..XXX"
        BITMAP "..XX...X"
        BITMAP "..X.X.X"
        BITMAP "..X....X"
        BITMAP ".X.....X"
        BITMAP ".X....X."
        BITMAP ".X....X."
        BITMAP ".X....X."
        BITMAP ".XXX..X."
        BITMAP "....XXX."
        BITMAP "........"
        BITMAP "........"

        BITMAP "........"  ' 10 degrees
        BITMAP "........"
        BITMAP "..XX...."
        BITMAP "..X.XX.."
        BITMAP "..X...XX"
        BITMAP "..XX...X"
        BITMAP "..X..X.X"
        BITMAP "..X...,X"
        BITMAP ".X.....X"
        BITMAP ".X.....X"
        BITMAP ".X....X."
        BITMAP ".X....X."
        BITMAP ".XX...X."
        BITMAP "...XX.X."
        BITMAP ".....XX."
        BITMAP "........"
```

But unfortunately this would require a lot of pages (one page for each group of 3 sprites), so we had to list it in compressed form using DATA. Here comes the real *smiley.bas*:

```
smiley_bitmaps:
    DATA $0000,$3e00,$2222,$2236 ' 0 degrees
    DATA $2222,$2222,$3e22,$0000

    DATA $0000,$3800,$3127,$2125 ' 5 degrees
    DATA $4241,$4242,$0e72,$0000
```

```
DATA $0000,$2c30,$3123,$2125 ' 10 degrees
DATA $4141,$4242,$1a62,$0006

DATA $0000,$3820,$3126,$4125 ' 15 degrees
DATA $4141,$4242,$0e32,$0002

DATA $0000,$1810,$3116,$2321 ' 20 degrees
DATA $4222,$4242,$1c24,$0004

DATA $0000,$1810,$3214,$2321 ' 25 degrees
DATA $4221,$2242,$0c12,$0004

DATA $1000,$1418,$2a24,$2321 ' 30 degrees
DATA $4241,$2242,$1412,$040c

DATA $1000,$1818,$2a24,$2322 ' 35 degrees
DATA $4141,$2222,$0a12,$040c

DATA $0800,$140c,$1a12,$2121 ' 40 degrees
DATA $4243,$2222,$1414,$0808

DATA $0800,$1408,$2a14,$4122 ' 45 degrees
DATA $4143,$2222,$1414,$0808

DATA $0800,$1408,$2a14,$4222 ' 50 degrees
DATA $2143,$1221,$1412,$080c

DATA $0400,$0a0c,$2a12,$4122 ' 55 degrees
DATA $2341,$2222,$1824,$1018

DATA $0400,$140c,$2a12,$4242 ' 60 degrees
DATA $2341,$2221,$1424,$1018

DATA $0000,$0c04,$2612,$4242 ' 65 degrees
DATA $2321,$2221,$1814,$0010

DATA $0000,$0c04,$4634,$4242 ' 70 degrees
DATA $2322,$2121,$1c12,$0010

DATA $0000,$0e02,$4632,$4142 ' 75 degrees
DATA $4141,$2125,$3826,$0020

DATA $0000,$1a06,$4662,$4142 ' 80 degrees
DATA $2141,$2125,$2c23,$0030

DATA $0000,$0e00,$4672,$4242 ' 85 degrees
DATA $2141,$2125,$3827,$0000
```

```
DATA $0000,$3e00,$2222,$2226 ' 90 degrees
DATA $2222,$2226,$3e22,$0000

DATA $0000,$3800,$2127,$2125 ' 95 degrees
DATA $4241,$4642,$0e72,$0000

DATA $0000,$2c30,$2123,$2125 ' 100 degrees
DATA $4141,$4642,$1a62,$0006

DATA $0000,$3820,$2126,$4125 ' 105 degrees
DATA $4141,$4642,$0e32,$0002

DATA $0000,$1810,$2116,$2321 ' 110 degrees
DATA $4222,$4642,$1c24,$0004

DATA $0000,$1810,$2214,$2321 ' 115 degrees
DATA $4221,$2642,$0c12,$0004

DATA $1000,$1418,$2224,$2321 ' 120 degrees
DATA $4241,$2a42,$1412,$040c

DATA $1000,$1818,$2224,$2322 ' 125 degrees
DATA $4141,$2a22,$0a12,$040c

DATA $0800,$140c,$1212,$2121 ' 130 degrees
DATA $4243,$2a22,$1414,$0808

DATA $0800,$1408,$2214,$4122 ' 135 degrees
DATA $4143,$2a22,$1414,$0808

DATA $0800,$1408,$2214,$4222 ' 140 degrees
DATA $2143,$1a21,$1412,$080c

DATA $0400,$0a0c,$2212,$4122 ' 145 degrees
DATA $2341,$2a22,$1824,$1018

DATA $0400,$140c,$2212,$4242 ' 150 degrees
DATA $2341,$2a21,$1424,$1018

DATA $0000,$0c04,$2212,$4242 ' 155 degrees
DATA $2321,$3221,$1814,$0010

DATA $0000,$0c04,$4234,$4242 ' 160 degrees
DATA $2322,$3121,$1c12,$0010

DATA $0000,$0e02,$4232,$4142 ' 165 degrees
DATA $4141,$3125,$3826,$0020
```

```
DATA $0000,$1a06,$4262,$4142 ' 170 degrees
DATA $2141,$3125,$2c23,$0030

DATA $0000,$0e00,$4272,$4242 ' 175 degrees
DATA $2141,$3125,$3827,$0000

DATA $0000,$3e00,$2222,$2222 ' 180 degrees
DATA $2222,$2236,$3e22,$0000

DATA $0000,$3800,$2127,$2121 ' 185 degrees
DATA $4241,$4652,$0e72,$0000

DATA $0000,$2c30,$2123,$2121 ' 190 degrees
DATA $4141,$4652,$1a62,$0006

DATA $0000,$3820,$2126,$4121 ' 195 degrees
DATA $4141,$4652,$0e32,$0002

DATA $0000,$1810,$2116,$2121 ' 200 degrees
DATA $6222,$4642,$1c24,$0004

DATA $0000,$1810,$2214,$2121 ' 205 degrees
DATA $6221,$2642,$0c12,$0004

DATA $1000,$1418,$2224,$2121 ' 210 degrees
DATA $6241,$2a42,$1412,$040c

DATA $1000,$1818,$2224,$2122 ' 215 degrees
DATA $6141,$2a22,$0a12,$040c

DATA $0800,$140c,$1212,$2121 ' 220 degrees
DATA $4261,$2a22,$1414,$0808

DATA $0800,$1408,$2214,$4122 ' 225 degrees
DATA $4161,$2a22,$1414,$0808

DATA $0800,$1408,$2214,$4222 ' 230 degrees
DATA $2161,$1a21,$1412,$080c

DATA $0400,$0a0c,$2212,$6122 ' 235 degrees
DATA $2141,$2a22,$1824,$1018

DATA $0400,$140c,$2212,$6242 ' 240 degrees
DATA $2141,$2a21,$1424,$1018

DATA $0000,$0c04,$2212,$6242 ' 245 degrees
DATA $2121,$3221,$1814,$0010
```

```
DATA $0000,$0c04,$4234,$6242 ' 250 degrees
DATA $2122,$3121,$1c12,$0010

DATA $0000,$0e02,$4232,$4152 ' 255 degrees
DATA $4141,$3121,$3826,$0020

DATA $0000,$1a06,$4262,$4152 ' 260 degrees
DATA $2141,$3121,$2c23,$0030

DATA $0000,$0e00,$4272,$4252 ' 265 degrees
DATA $2141,$3121,$3827,$0000

DATA $0000,$3e00,$2222,$2232 ' 270 degrees
DATA $2222,$2232,$3e22,$0000

DATA $0000,$3800,$3127,$2121 ' 275 degrees
DATA $4241,$4252,$0e72,$0000

DATA $0000,$2c30,$3123,$2121 ' 280 degrees
DATA $4141,$4252,$1a62,$0006

DATA $0000,$3820,$3126,$4121 ' 285 degrees
DATA $4141,$4252,$0e32,$0002

DATA $0000,$1810,$3116,$2121 ' 290 degrees
DATA $6222,$4242,$1c24,$0004

DATA $0000,$1810,$3214,$2121 ' 295 degrees
DATA $6221,$2242,$0c12,$0004

DATA $1000,$1418,$2a24,$2121 ' 300 degrees
DATA $6241,$2242,$1412,$040c

DATA $1000,$1818,$2a24,$2122 ' 305 degrees
DATA $6141,$2222,$0a12,$040c

DATA $0800,$140c,$1a12,$2121 ' 310 degrees
DATA $4261,$2222,$1414,$0808

DATA $0800,$1408,$2a14,$4122 ' 315 degrees
DATA $4161,$2222,$1414,$0808

DATA $0800,$1408,$2a14,$4222 ' 320 degrees
DATA $2161,$1221,$1412,$080c

DATA $0400,$0a0c,$2a12,$6122 ' 325 degrees
DATA $2141,$2222,$1824,$1018
```

```
    DATA $0400,$140c,$2a12,$6242 ' 330 degrees
    DATA $2141,$2221,$1424,$1018

    DATA $0000,$0c04,$2612,$6242 ' 335 degrees
    DATA $2121,$2221,$1814,$0010

    DATA $0000,$0c04,$4634,$6242 ' 340 degrees
    DATA $2122,$2121,$1c12,$0010

    DATA $0000,$0e02,$4632,$4152 ' 345 degrees
    DATA $4141,$2121,$3826,$0020

    DATA $0000,$1a06,$4662,$4152 ' 350 degrees
    DATA $2141,$2121,$2c23,$0030

    DATA $0000,$0e00,$4672,$4252 ' 355 degrees
    DATA $2141,$2121,$3827,$0000

sin:
    DATA -64,-64,-63,-62,-60,-58,-55,-52
    DATA -49,-45,-41,-37,-32,-27,-22,-17
    DATA -11,-6,0,6,11,17,22,27
    DATA 32,37,41,45,49,52,55,58
    DATA 60,62,63,64,64,64,63,62
    DATA 60,58,55,52,49,45,41,37
    DATA 32,27,22,17,11,6,0,-6
    DATA -11,-17,-22,-27,-32,-37,-41,-45
    DATA -49,-52,-55,-58,-60,-62,-63,-64
```

As you can see above, there is also a sine table in 5 degrees steps, in which each value is represented as a fixed-point 10.6-bit value (10 bits for integer side and 6 bits for fraction).

Another feature from IntyBASIC is the easiness of accessing data. For example, in the code "sin(2)", the "2" is the index used to access the table "sin" and fetch the value in memory, in this case -63. But that doesn't mean the language actually implements the mathematical sine function, the syntax just looks like it does.

## 7.3 The level

This game has only one level but it's a nice challenge. We are going to describe it column by column (the game scrolls to the right).

We have 4 different tiles: 0 (empty), 1 (floor), 2 (platform) and 3 (obstacle, e.g. instant death).

We need to fill 12 rows on each screen refresh frame, and we aren't going to put a single DATA 0,0,0,0,0,0,0,0,0,1,1,1,1 for each column, that would be too cumbersome, a waste of space and probably wouldn't fit into the Intellivision standard cartridge memory space.

How can we compact the level representation enough to make the game fit in the available cartridge memory? The answer: Repeat counts.

Each column has a repeat count, and inside each column, there is a repeat count for each tile to be shown. A zero in repeat count means the end of the column.

So the previous DATA shown can be compressed down to DATA 1,$8041,$0000

This formula means "repeat this column one time with eight 0 tiles, four 1 tiles, and then finish."

You want to extend it to two screens? That's easy, just replace the first 1 for 40 (20 * 2), meaning 40 columns (or 2 horizontal screens). This doesn't require additional data storage space.

So lets us add this at the end of our main file (after *INCLUDE* "*bouncy_title.bas*"):

```
    '
    ' Color for smiley and shadows
    '
smiley_colors:
    DATA $0807, $0806, $0806, $1801, $1801, $1801, $1801, $0800


    '
    ' Cards used to draw level
    ' 0 = Empty background
    ' 1 = Floor
    ' 2 = Platform
```

```
     ' 3 = Obstacle
     '
card:
    DATA $0200
    DATA $1A07 + 16 * 8
    DATA $0A07 + 17 * 8
    DATA $0A05 + 18 * 8


    '
    ' Level data.
    ' First item is repeat count.
    ' Then a list is read until a byte is zero.
    '
    ' The left half of a byte indicates the row count.
    ' The right half of a byte indicates the card type.
    '
level_1_data:
    DATA 20,$9031,$0000
    DATA 1,$8013,$3100
    DATA 6,$9031,$0000
    DATA 2,$8013,$3100
    DATA 30,$9031,$0000
    DATA 3,$7011,$1300
    DATA 3,$9031,$0000
    DATA 3,$6011,$1013,$0000
    DATA 3,$9031,$0000
    DATA 3,$5011,$2013,$0000
    DATA 3,$9031,$0000
    DATA 3,$4011,$3013,$0000
    DATA 14,$7051,$0000
    DATA 2,$6013,$4100
    DATA 8,$7051,$0000
    DATA 2,$6013,$4100
    DATA 8,$7051,$0000
    DATA 2,$6013,$4100
    DATA 14,$7051,$0000
    DATA 3,$5011,$2013,$0000
    DATA 3,$9031,$0000
    DATA 3,$4011,$3013,$0000
    DATA 14,$7051,$0000
    DATA 2,$6013,$4100
    DATA 8,$7051,$0000
    DATA 2,$6013,$4100
    DATA 8,$7051,$0000
    DATA 2,$6013,$4100
    DATA 8,$7051,$0000


    DATA 12,$9031,$0000
```

```
DATA 3,$7012,$1331,$0000
DATA 3,$6012,$1013,$3100
DATA 3,$7012,$1331,$0000
DATA 3,$6012,$1013,$3100
DATA 3,$7012,$1331,$0000
DATA 3,$6012,$1013,$3100
DATA 3,$7012,$1331,$0000
DATA 12,$9031,$0000

DATA 12,$9031,$0000
DATA 3,$7012,$1331,$0000
DATA 3,$6012,$1013,$3100
DATA 3,$5012,$2013,$3100
DATA 3,$4012,$3013,$3100
DATA 3,$5012,$2013,$3100
DATA 3,$6012,$1013,$3100
DATA 3,$7012,$1331,$0000
DATA 12,$9031,$0000

DATA 12,$9031,$0000
DATA 3,$7012,$1331,$0000
DATA 3,$6012,$1013,$3100
DATA 3,$7012,$1331,$0000
DATA 3,$6012,$1013,$3100
DATA 3,$7012,$1331,$0000
DATA 3,$6012,$1013,$3100
DATA 3,$7012,$1331,$0000
DATA 12,$9031,$0000

DATA 12,$9031,$0000
DATA 3,$7012,$1331,$0000
DATA 3,$6012,$1013,$3100
DATA 3,$5012,$2013,$3100
DATA 3,$4012,$3013,$3100
DATA 3,$5012,$2013,$3100
DATA 3,$6012,$1013,$3100
DATA 3,$7012,$1331,$0000
DATA 12,$9031,$0000

DATA 12,$9031,$0000
DATA 1,$8013,$3100
DATA 4,$9031,$0000
DATA 2,$8013,$3100
DATA 12,$9031,$0000
DATA 1,$8013,$3100
DATA 4,$9031,$0000
DATA 2,$8013,$3100
DATA 12,$9031,$0000
```

```
        DATA 1,$8013,$3100
        DATA 4,$9031,$0000
        DATA 2,$8013,$3100
        DATA 40,$9031,$0000

        DATA 255,$9031,$0000

        '
        ' Bitmaps used by the game
        '
game_bitmaps:
        BITMAP "XXXXXXXX"
        BITMAP "X...X..."
        BITMAP "X...X..."
        BITMAP "X...X..."
        BITMAP "XXXXXXXX"
        BITMAP "X...X..."
        BITMAP "X...X..."
        BITMAP "X...X..."

        BITMAP "XXXXXXXX"
        BITMAP ".X.X.X,X"
        BITMAP "X.X.X.X."
        BITMAP "XXXXXXXX"
        BITMAP "........"
        BITMAP "........"
        BITMAP "........"
        BITMAP "........"

        BITMAP "XXXXXXXX"
        BITMAP "XXXXX.X"
        BITMAP "XX.X.X.X"
        BITMAP "XXX.XX.X"
        BITMAP "XX.X.X.X"
        BITMAP "XXXXX.X"
        BITMAP "X......X"
        BITMAP "XXXXXXXX"

        '
        ' The smiley face generated "auto-magically"
        '
        INCLUDE "smiley.bas"
```

The level data illustrated here extends over 460 columns (460 / 20 = 94 screens of level data!)

The scrolling speed is two pixels per frame, so every four frames the SCROLL function will move forward by a full column. This means 460 / (60 / 4) = 30 seconds of gameplay. Friendly reminder: 60 is the number of video frames per second on an NTSC Intellivision.

Let us add the code to show the initial screen of the level. Replace *WHILE 1: WEND* with this:

```
    '
    ' Start new game
    '
    CLS
    MODE 1
    WAIT
    DEFINE 16,3,game_bitmaps
    WAIT
    FOR c = 0 TO 14 STEP 2
        DEFINE c,2,smiley_bitmaps
        WAIT
    NEXT c

    lives = 2

    CLS
    BORDER 0,3
    WAIT

    '
    ' Restart game entry point
    '
restart:

    '
    ' Draw start screen using level data
    '
    #level_offset = VARPTR level_1_data(0)
    repeat_count = 0

    column = 0
    DO
        GOSUB draw_column
        column = column + 1
    LOOP WHILE column < 20

    '
    ' Setup player and shadow
    '
```

```
      smiley_y = 64
      smiley_frame = 0
      jump = 0
      FOR c = 0 TO 7
          sx(c) = SMILEY_X
          sy(c) = smiley_y
      NEXT c

      '
      ' Setup scroll
      '
      offset_x = 0
      offset_y = 0
      offset_d = 0

      WHILE 1: WEND

      '
      ' Draw a new column from level
      '
draw_column: PROCEDURE

      '
      ' Should it be repeating the last column?
      '
      IF repeat_count > 1 THEN
          repeat_count = repeat_count - 1
          #level_offset = #repeat_offset
      ELSE
          repeat_count = PEEK(#level_offset)
          #level_offset = #level_offset + 1
          #repeat_offset = #level_offset
      END IF

      d = column
      WHILE 1

          '
          ' Read one word from level
          '
          #word = PEEK(#level_offset)
          #level_offset = #level_offset + 1

          '
          ' Unpack high byte
          '
          c = #word / 256
          IF c = 0 THEN RETURN
```

```
          #c = card(c AND $0f)
          DO
               #backtab(d) = #c
               d = d + 20
               c = c - $10
          LOOP WHILE c >= $10


          '
          ' Unpack low byte
          '
          c = #word AND $FF
          IF c = 0 THEN RETURN
          #c = card(c AND $0f)
          DO
               #backtab(d) = #c
               d = d + 20
               c = c - $10
          LOOP WHILE c >= $10
     WEND
     END
```

Now we can start the game and see the initial screen of the wide band composing the level.

Notice how the variable *#level_offset* contains the pointer to the level data. This pointer is obtained by using another feature of IntyBASIC called *VARPTR*. This allows us to get the location of a variable or an array, essentially the address where it's located.

Then to read the level data we use the *PEEK(expr)* syntax which reads the data from that memory location.

## 7.4 Scrolling the level

Now it's time to make the level scroll. Let us add the main game loop replacing the *WHILE 1: WEND*

```
     '
     ' Main game loop
     '
game_loop:
     IF offset_x = 0 THEN     ' Is it required a new column?
```

```
        offset_d = 2: offset_x = 8 - SPEED
    ELSE
        offset_x = offset_x - SPEED
    END IF

    SCROLL offset_x, offset_y, offset_d

    WAIT        ' Synchronize

    offset_d = 0
    IF offset_x = 8 - SPEED THEN' New column required
        column = 19
        GOSUB draw_column
    END IF

    IF repeat_count = 255 THEN    ' Completed level?
        PLAY OFF
        PRINT AT 45 COLOR $0207,"CHAMPION!"
        FOR c = 0 TO 240
            WAIT
        NEXT c
        GOTO title_screen
    END IF

    GOTO game_loop
```

The variable *offset_x* is displaced by the *SPEED* constant (which is 2). When it completes a card, it sets *offset_d* to 2 to indicate to IntyBASIC to do a full screen scroll by one card to the left and then inserts a new column on the right side of the screen.

This allows us to traverse the whole level, and at the end we'll be rewarded with the triumphant phrase"Champion!".

# 7.5 The player

Now comes in the important part, namely the player. He can move across the level and jump over obstacles.

We're going to use all 8 sprites of the Intellivision in order to show a shadow for the player when jumping or falling.

Add this on the line before the *SCROLL* statement:

```
    GOSUB update_sprites
```

Now, add this after *GOTO game_loop*:

```
    '
    ' Update sprites
    '
update_sprites:        PROCEDURE

    '
    ' Handle shadow, it appears when jumping or falling
    '
    IF sy(7) <> sy(6) THEN sx(7) = sx(6) - SPEED ELSE sx(7) = sx(6)
    IF sy(6) <> sy(5) THEN sx(6) = sx(5) - SPEED ELSE sx(6) = sx(5)
    IF sy(5) <> sy(4) THEN sx(5) = sx(4) - SPEED ELSE sx(5) = sx(4)
    IF sy(4) <> sy(3) THEN sx(4) = sx(3) - SPEED ELSE sx(4) = sx(3)
    IF sy(3) <> sy(2) THEN sx(3) = sx(2) - SPEED ELSE sx(3) = sx(2)
    IF sy(2) <> sy(1) THEN sx(2) = sx(1) - SPEED ELSE sx(2) = sx(1)
    IF sy(1) <> sy(0) THEN sx(1) = sx(0) - SPEED ELSE sx(1) = sx(0)
    sy(7) = sy(6)
    sy(6) = sy(5)
    sy(5) = sy(4)
    sy(4) = sy(3)
    sy(3) = sy(2)
    sy(2) = sy(1)
    sy(1) = sy(0)
    sx(0) = SMILEY_X
    sy(0) = smiley_y


    '
    ' Update sprites
    '
    d = next_sprite * 8
    FOR c = 0 TO 7
        IF sy(c) THEN
            SPRITE c, $0308 + sx(c) - offset_x, $0088 + sy(c) -
offset_y, smiley_colors(c) + d
        ELSE
            SPRITE c, 0
        END IF
        d = (d - 16) AND $7F
    NEXT c

    '
    ' Define current look of player
    ' Notice it preserves the old sprites for shadow
```

110

```
'
DEFINE next_sprite,2,VARPTR smiley_bitmaps(smiley_frame * 8)
next_sprite = (next_sprite + 2) AND $0F
END
```

The logic behind this code moves the latest position in a pipeline using arrays *sx* and *sy*, so the previous positions of the player are shown like a trail.

While it's doing the setup of sprites for displaying, the code uses the data from *smiley_colors* to select the different colors for the player and shadow. Also, notice the constant $0088 to select 8x16 sprites but at half-height. If you want to experiment, try the different zoom sizes: $0188, $0288 and $0388.

Notice that the program keeps track of the current defined sprite in variable *next_sprite* so that each sprite keeps its defined graphics, and the most current one is the "pointed" one as defined at the end of the procedure.

The corresponding graphic is located by using *VARPTR*. Usually, each 8x8 pixels card corresponds to 8 *BITMAP* statements, equivalent to 4 words of memory, but here we're using 8x16 pixel sprites, so it's double the data (8 words of memory). So *smiley_frame * 8* is the index inside the *smiley_bitmaps* array and *VARPTR* allows us to get the position.

There is only one control method in this game: jumping, by pressing the disc.

Let us insert the logic for player jumping on the row before *GOTO game_loop*.

```
'
' Handle jump physics
'
IF jump THEN
    smiley_frame = smiley_frame + 1
    c = jump - 1
    IF c < 9 THEN ' Going up
        smiley_y = smiley_y + sin(c * 2) / 16
    ELSE ' Going down
```

```
                smiley_y = smiley_y - sin((17 - c) * 2) / 16
        END IF
        jump = jump + 1
        IF jump = 19 THEN jump = 0

            '

        ' Check if it falls over something
            '

        IF (smiley_y AND 7) < 3 THEN
            #c = #backtab(20 + SMILEY_X / 8 + smiley_y / 8 * 20)
            IF #c = card(1) THEN    ' Floor
                smiley_y = (smiley_y / 8) * 8
                smiley_frame = (smiley_frame + 17) / 18 * 18
                jump = 0
            ELSEIF #c = card(2) THEN    ' Platform
                smiley_y = (smiley_y / 8) * 8
                smiley_frame = (smiley_frame + 17) / 18 * 18
                jump = 0
            ELSEIF #c = card(3) THEN     ' Obstacle
                GOTO lost_life
            END IF
        END IF
        IF smiley_frame = 72 THEN smiley_frame = 0
    ELSE

            '
        ' Check horizontal collision
            '

        IF offset_x = 0 THEN
            #c = #backtab(SMILEY_X / 8 + 1 + smiley_y / 8 * 20)
            IF #c = card(3) THEN GOTO lost_life
        END IF


            '
        ' Check fall possibility
            '

        #c = #backtab(20 + SMILEY_X / 8 + smiley_y / 8 * 20)
        IF #c = card(0) THEN
            smiley_y = smiley_y + 2
        ELSEIF #c = card(3) THEN
            GOTO lost_life
        END IF
    END IF

    '
' Read controller
    '
c = CONT
```

```
        d = c AND $E0
        IF (d = $80) + (d = $40) + (d = $20) THEN
              ' Ignore keypad
        ELSEIF (c AND $1F) <> 0 THEN ' Disc pressed
              IF jump = 0 THEN
                    jump = 1
                    sound_effect = 1: sound_state = 0
              END IF
        END IF
```

Before this code can work, we need to add this piece of code on the
line after *GOTO game_loop*.

```
      '
      ' Player lost a life
      '
lost_life:
      PLAY OFF
      sound_effect = 2: sound_state = 0
      IF lives = 0 THEN   ' No more lives
            FOR count = 0 TO 240
                  PRINT AT 65 COLOR $0202 + (count AND 4),"GAME  OVER"
                  IF count < 30 THEN ' Tremble
                        c = RAND
                        SCROLL c AND 3, (c / 8) AND 3
                  ELSE
                        SCROLL 0,0
                  END IF
                  WAIT
            NEXT count
            GOTO title_screen
      END IF


      '
      ' One life less
      '
      lives = lives - 1
      FOR count = 0 TO 120
            PRINT AT 67 COLOR $0203 + (count AND 4),"OOUCH!"
            IF count < 30 THEN ' Small tremble
                  c = RAND
                  SCROLL c AND 1, (c / 8) AND 1
            ELSE
                  SCROLL 0,0
            END IF
            WAIT
```

```
NEXT count
GOTO restart
```

While the player isn't jumping, the code checks for collisions in horizontal and the possibility of falling into the void.

The control code only monitors the pressing of the disc in order to trigger the jump function using the variable *jump*.

The jumping uses 18 frames. On each frame, the player turns 5 degrees to the right, so when the jump is finished, the player has turned 90 degrees.

In case of landing before the end of a jump, the player is adjusted automatically to 90 degrees (the expression *(smiley_frame + 17) / 18 * 18)*.

The *#backtab* is checked periodically with the current coordinates to check for collisions. Notice how it takes the Y coordinate, divided by 8 and multiplies it by 20 to get the card column, and then adds the X coordinate divided by 8 to get the proper position, plus offsets depending on where it checks (ahead horizontally or below vertically).

When a life is lost, the screen trembles slightly and the trembling is stronger when the game is lost.

# 7.6 Explosion

The game is technically complete, but why not add some bells and whistles? Let us implement an explosion effect when the player crashes.

Insert this code after the *lost_life:* label.

```
FOR c = 0 TO 7
    sx(c) = SMILEY_X
    sy(c) = smiley_y
NEXT c
```

This sets up all the sprites to point to the current position.

Now add this line after each one of the two *PRINT* statements inside the *lost_life:* label:

```
GOSUB cube_explosion
```

Now put the *cube_explosion* procedure just after the line saying *GOTO restart.*

```
    '
    ' Cube explosion using all sprites
    '
cube_explosion:    PROCEDURE
    FOR c = 0 TO 7
        SPRITE c, $0308 + sx(c) - offset_x, $0108 + sy(c) -
offset_y, $0077
        IF c < 2 THEN ' Left side
            sx(c) = sx(c) - RANDOM(3)
        ELSEIF c < 4 THEN
            sx(c) = sx(c) - RANDOM(2)
        ELSEIF c < 6 THEN
            sx(c) = sx(c) + RANDOM(2)
        ELSE ' Right side
            sx(c) = sx(c) + RANDOM(3)
        END IF
        IF count > 15 THEN ' Falling
            IF sy(c) < 96 THEN sy(c) = sy(c) + (count - 8) / 8
        ELSE ' Exploding
            sy(c) = sy(c) - RANDOM(2) - (15 - count) / 8
        END IF
    NEXT c
    END
```

All the sprites are used to show white particles (recreated using the period character from the Intellivision GROM, a period is $0e * 8 = $0070 + 7 white = $0077)

The leftmost pixels move more to the left than the center ones, and the rightmost pixels move more to the right than the center ones. So the explosion "expands". And using the *count* variable, the code checks if the particles should rise or fall.

## 7.7 Sound effects

Just like in the previous games, it's time to implement sound effects. Only two sound effects are needed for this game: One for jumping and another for the explosion.

These are already set up using *sound_effect* and *sound_state*.

Let us add this line at the start of the game code:

```
ON FRAME GOSUB play_effects
```

It calls the sound player upon each video frame.

Now let us add the corresponding code at the end of the game code:

```
'
' Play sound effects
'
play_effects: PROCEDURE
    ON sound_effect GOSUB sound_none, sound_jump, sound_explosion
    END


    '
    ' No sound effect
    '
sound_none:   PROCEDURE
    SOUND 2,,0
    SOUND 4,,$38
    END


    '
    ' Jumping sound effect
    '
sound_jump:   PROCEDURE
    SOUND 2,100 - sound_state * 8,12
    SOUND 4,,$38
    sound_state = sound_state + 1
    IF sound_state = 9 THEN sound_effect = 0
    END


    '
    ' Explosion sound effect
    '
sound_explosion:   PROCEDURE
    SOUND 2,,15-sound_state / 8
```

```
    SOUND 4,31 - sound_state / 2,$1c
    sound_state = sound_state + 1
    IF sound_state = 28 THEN sound_effect = 0
    END
```

The jumping sound works by changing the frequency to be more acute, while the explosion sound works exclusively with the noise channel starting with a low frequency and then goes to a higher frequency for white-noise, plus a volume adjustment to make it feel like it's dissipating.

## 7.8 Music

So far none of the games we made have music but let this one be an exception. We'll be using the music from an example included with IntyBASIC *music.bas*.

Add this to the end of the game code:

```
music_game:
    DATA 5
    MUSIC G5#Y,C3#,-,M1
    MUSIC S,S,-,M2
    MUSIC F5#,G3#,-,M2
    MUSIC S,S,-,M2
    MUSIC E5,C3#,-,M1
    MUSIC S,S,-,M2
    MUSIC D5#,G3#,-,M2
    MUSIC S,S,-,M2
    MUSIC E5,C3#,-,M1
    MUSIC S,S,-,M2
    MUSIC F5#,G3#,-,M2
    MUSIC S,S,-,M2
    MUSIC G5#,C3#,-,M1
    MUSIC S,S,-,M2
    MUSIC S,G3#,-,M2
    MUSIC S,S,-,M2
    MUSIC S,C3#,-,M1
    MUSIC S,S,-,M2
    MUSIC C5#,G3#,-,M2
    MUSIC -,S,-,M2
    MUSIC G5#,C3#,-,M1
    MUSIC S,S,-,M2
```

```
MUSIC E5,G3#,-,M2
MUSIC -,S,-,M2
MUSIC F5#,B2,-,M1
MUSIC S,S,-,M2
MUSIC S,F3#,-,M2
MUSIC S,S,-,M2
MUSIC S,B2,-,M1
MUSIC S,S,-,M2
MUSIC -,F3#,-,M2
MUSIC -,S,-,M2
MUSIC -,B2,-,M1
MUSIC -,S,-,M2
MUSIC -,F3#,-,M2
MUSIC -,S,-,M2
MUSIC -,B2,-,M1
MUSIC -,S,-,M2
MUSIC -,F3#,-,M1
MUSIC -,S,-,M2
MUSIC C5#,B2,-,M1
MUSIC S,S,-,M2
MUSIC F5#,F3#,-,M1
MUSIC S,S,-,M2
MUSIC C5#,B2,-,M1
MUSIC S,S,-,M2
MUSIC E5,A2,-,M1
MUSIC S,S,-,M2
MUSIC S,E3,-,M1
MUSIC S,S,-,M2
MUSIC S,A2,-,M1
MUSIC S,S,-,M2
MUSIC S,E3,-,M1
MUSIC S,S,-,M2
MUSIC S,A2,-,M1
MUSIC S,S,-,M2
MUSIC S,E3,-,M1
MUSIC S,S,-,M2
MUSIC S,A2,-,M1
MUSIC S,S,-,M2
MUSIC F5#,E3,-,M1
MUSIC S,S,-,M2
MUSIC E5,A2,-,M2
MUSIC S,S,-,M2
MUSIC D5#,E3,-,M1
MUSIC S,S,-,M2
MUSIC S,A2,-,M2
MUSIC S,S,-,M2
MUSIC C5,G2#,-,M1
MUSIC S,S,-,M2
```

```
MUSIC S,D3#,-,M2
MUSIC S,S,-,M2
MUSIC S,G2#,-,M1
MUSIC S,S,-,M2
MUSIC S,D3#,-,M2
MUSIC S,S,-,M2
MUSIC S,G2#,-,M1
MUSIC S,S,-,M2
MUSIC -,D3#,-,M2
MUSIC -,S,-,M2
MUSIC -,G2#,-,M1
MUSIC -,S,-,M2
MUSIC -,D3#,-,M2
MUSIC -,S,-,M2
MUSIC -,G2#,-,M1
MUSIC -,S,-,M2
MUSIC -,D3#,-,M1
MUSIC -,S,-,M3
MUSIC -,G2#,-,M1
MUSIC -,S,-,M2
MUSIC -,D3#,-,M1
MUSIC -,S,-,M3
MUSIC -,G2#,-,M1
MUSIC -,S,-,M1
MUSIC -,D3#,-,M1
MUSIC -,S,-,M1
MUSIC REPEAT
```

And start the music on the line after *restart_label:*

```
PLAY music_game          ' Start music
```

And voilà! The game has music, adding some playability quality.

# Chapter 8

## Assembly language

Let's take a closer (and brief) look at the CP1610 processor used in the Intellivision.

The CP1610 processor has 8 main registers and 1 status register. The 8 main registers contain 16 bits. The status register has Sign, Overflow, Zero and Carry status bits:

|  | Special function |
|---|---|
| R0 | None |
| R1 | None |
| R2 | None |
| R3 | None |
| R4 | Autoincrement |
| R5 | Autoincrement |
| R6 | Stack Pointer (autoincrement on writing, predecrement on reading) |
| R7 | Program Counter |
| SWD (Status WorD) | Processor status flags |

The autoincrement/predecrement only happens when using the register to access memory (instructions with the "@" character in the name). Note the register R0 cannot be use to access memory.

The Intellivision contains a EXEC ROM memory that is executed on power-on or reset, and at the end of the boot sequence, the CPU jumps to address $5000 (or possibly $4800), which is where the first byte of the cartridge software is located.

The instructions are read from memory and executed sequentially until the processor finds a branch instruction to "jump" to another part of the code. These branch instructions can be unconditional (always jump) or conditional (jump if a register flag is set to a certain value).

The instruction set provided by the CP1610 is as follows:

| Instruction | Flags affected | Operation |
|---|---|---|
| ADCR rd | S,Z,C,OV | Add carry flag to rd. |
| ADD sa,rd | S,Z,C,OV | Add from address to rd. |
| ADD@ rs,rd | S,Z,C,OV | Add from address pointed by rs to rd. |
| ADDI #sa,rd | S,Z,C,OV | Add immediate (PC+1) to rd. |
| ADDR rs,rd | S,Z,C,OV | Add rs to rd. |
| AND sa,rd | S,Z | Logical AND from address to rd. |
| AND@ rs,rd | S,Z | Logical AND from address pointed by rs to rd. |
| ANDI #sa,rd | S,Z | Logical AND immediate (PC+1) to rd. |
| ANDR rs,rd | S,Z | Logical AND of rs to rd. |
| B da | | Branch unconditional (-1025 to 1024 words) from PC+2. |
| BC/BLGE da | | Branch if carry (C) set. |
| BEGIN | | Equivalent to PSHR R5. |
| BEQ/BZE da | | Branch if zero (Z) set (equal). |
| BESC da | | Branch if equal sign and carry. (S^C)=0. |

| Instruction | Flags affected | Operation |
| --- | --- | --- |
| BGE/BNLT da | | Branch if greater than or equal signed (S^OV=0). |
| BGT/BNLE da | | Branch if greater than or equal signed ZI(S^OV)=0. |
| BLE/BNGT da | | Branch if less than signed ZI(S^OV)=1. |
| BL addr | | Equivalent to JSR R5,addr. |
| BLT/BNGE da | | Branch if less than signed (S^OV=1). |
| BMI da | | Branch if sign (S) set. |
| BNC/BLLT da | | Branch if carry (C) clear. |
| BNE/BNZE da | | Branch if zero (Z) clear (not equal). |
| BNOV da | | Branch if overflow (OV) clear. |
| BOV da | | Branch if overflow (OV) set. |
| BPL da | | Branch if sign (S) clear. |
| BUSC da | | Branch if unequal Sign and Carry. (S^C)=1. |
| CLRC | C | Clear carry to zero (non-interruptable). |
| CLRR rd | S,Z | Set rd to zero. |
| CMP sa,rd | S,Z,C,OV | Compare from address to rd. |
| CMP@ rs,rd | S,Z,C,OV | Compare from address pointed by rs to rd. |
| CMPI #sa,rd | S,Z,C,OV | Compare immediate (PC+1) to rd. |
| CMPR rs,rd | S,Z,C,OV | Compare rs to rd. |
| COMR rd | S,Z | One's complement rd bits. |
| DECR rd | S,Z | Decrement rd by 1. |

| Instruction | Flags affected | Operation |
|---|---|---|
| DIS | | Disable interrupts (non-interruptable). |
| EIS | | Enable interrupts (non-interruptable). |
| GSWD rd | | Copy SWD to rd. |
| HALT | | Halt after next interruptible instruction. |
| INCR rd | S,Z | Increment rd by 1. |
| J addr | | Jump to 16 bits address. |
| JD addr | | Jump to 16 bits address and disable interrupt system. |
| JE addr | | Jump to 16 bits address and enable interrupt system. |
| JR rs | S,Z | Jump to address contained in rs. |
| JSR bb,addr | | Jump to 16 bits address saving return address (PC+3 words) in bb. |
| JSRD bb,addr | | Jump to 16 bits address saving return address (PC+3 words) in bb. Disable interrupt system. |
| JSRE bb,addr | | Jump to 16 bits address saving return address (PC+3 words) in bb. Enable interrupt system. |
| MOVR rs,rd | S,Z | Move content of rs to rd. |
| MVI sa,rd | | Move from source address to rd. |
| MVI@ rs,rd | | Move data from address in rs to rd. |
| MVII #sa,rd | | Move immediate PC+1 to rd. |
| MVO rs,da | | Move from rs to destination address. |

| Instruction | Flags affected | Operation |
| --- | --- | --- |
| MVO@ rs,rd | | Move from rs to address in rd (autoincrement if necessary, not support rs=rd when r4,r5,r6 or r7). |
| MVOI rs,da | | Move from rs to PC+1 (da field). |
| NEGR rd | S,Z,C,OV | Two's complement of rd. |
| NOP | | No operation (one word). |
| NOPP | | No operation (two words). |
| PSHR rs | | Push data from rs to stack (equal to MVO@ rs,R6). |
| PULR rd | | Pop data from stack to rd (equal to MVI@ R6,rs). |
| RETURN | | Equivalent to PULR PC. |
| RLC rr,1 | S,Z,C | Rotate left rr by 1 bit through C. |
| RLC rr,2 | S,Z,C,OV | Rotate left rr by 2 bits through C, OV. |
| RRC rr,1 | S,Z,C | Rotate right rr by 1 bit, through C. |
| RRC rr,2 | S,Z,C,OV | Rotate right rr by 2 bits, through C, OV. |
| RSWD rs | S,Z,C,OV | Copy rs to SWD. |
| SAR rr,1 | S,Z | Shift arithmetic right rr by 1 bit. |
| SAR rr,2 | S,Z | Shift arithmetic right rr by 2 bits. |
| SARC rr,1 | S,Z,C | Shift arithmetic right rr by 1 bit, bit 0 goes into C. |
| SARC rr,2 | S,Z,C,OV | Shift arithmetic right rr by 2 bits, bit 0 goes into C, bit 1 goes into OV. |
| SDBD | | Set double byte data for next inst, must be a load/store instruction indirect (MVI@, ADD@ ...) or immediate (MVII, ADDI ...). Also cannot be a stack instruction (R6). |

| Instruction | Flags affected | Operation |
| --- | --- | --- |
| SETC | C | Set carry to one (non-interruptable). |
| SIN | | Software interrupt. It has no effect in Intellivision. |
| SLL rr,1 | S,Z | Shift left rr by 1 bit. |
| SLL rr,2 | S,Z | Shift left rr by 2 bits. |
| SLLC rr,1 | S,Z,C | Shift left rr by 1 bit. Bit 15 goes into C. |
| SLLC rr,2 | S,Z,C,OV | Shift left rr by 2 bits. Bit 15 goes into C. Bit 14 goes into OV. |
| SLR rr,1 | S,Z | Shift logical right rr by 1 bit. |
| SLR rr,2 | S,Z | Shift logical right rr by 2 bits. |
| SUB sa,rd | S,Z,C,OV | Substract address content from rd. |
| SUB@ rs,rd | S,Z,C,OV | Substract address pointed by rs from rd. |
| SUBI #sa,rd | S,Z,C,OV | Substract immediate (PC+1) from rd. |
| SUBR rs,rd | S,Z,C,OV | Substract rs from rd. |
| SWAP rr | S,Z | Swap bytes of rr. S equals bit 7. |
| TCI | | Terminate current interrupt (non-interruptable). |
| TSTR rs | S,Z | Test content of rs. |
| XOR sa,rd | S,Z | Logical XOR from address to rd. |
| XOR@ rs,rd | S,Z | Logical XOR from address pointed by rs to rd. |
| XORI #sa,rd | S,Z | Logical XOR immediate (PC+1) to rd. |
| XORR rs,rd | S,Z | Logical XOR of rs to rd. |

The abbreviation rd means register destination, rs is the register source, both means register 0 to 7. The abbreviation rr is linked to register 0-3. bb is linked to register 4-7. da means "displacement address". addr means "16-bit address".

So how fast can assembler be compared to IntyBASIC? Let's do some tests.

IntyBASIC allows us to integrate assembler directly using the ASM statement (for a single line of assembler) or the ASM INCLUDE statement (to insert an entire file composed of assembler statements during compilation).

First, here's an IntyBASIC program that shows 240 cards from the GROM memory of the Intellivision:

```
CLS

#base = FRAME

DO
     FOR c = 0 TO 239
          #backtab(c) = c * 8 + 7
     NEXT c
     d = d + 1
LOOP WHILE d < 100

#result = FRAME - #base
CLS
PRINT AT 0 COLOR 7,<>#result, " video frames"

WHILE 1: WEND
```

The program runs 100 times, displaying the 240 cards on the screen and then shows the time used to do the work.

This IntyBASIC program takes 204 frames to run, using jzintv with default NTSC settings.

Now let us rewrite the program with a routine in assembly language:

```
CLS
```

```
        #base = FRAME

        DO
              CALL accelerate
              d = d + 1
        LOOP WHILE d < 100

        #result = FRAME - #base
        CLS
        PRINT AT 0 COLOR 7,<>#result, " video frames"

        WHILE 1: WEND

        ASM ACCELERATE: PROC
        ASM   BEGIN
        ASM   MVII #7,R0
        ASM   MVII #8,R1
        ASM   MVII #7+240*8,R2
        ASM   MVII #$0200,R5
        ASM ACCELERATE1:
        ASM   MVO@ R0,R5
        ASM   ADDR R1,R0
        ASM   CMPR R2,R0
        ASM   BNE ACCELERATE1
        ASM   RETURN
        ASM   ENDP
```

It does the same work in only 60 video frames.

The assembler code was written to put the next card value in R0, the increment in R1 (8) and the limit in R2.

The internal loop moves the card to the screen (autoincrementing R5), adds the value R1 for the next card contained in R0 and does a comparison to check the boundary (R2 is the limit, R0 the current value) and jumps if not equal (BNE).

Notice the use of the **PROC** and **ENDP** directives of the as1600 assembler, these enclose the code and help to debug it by marking it clearly as a subroutine. The **BEGIN** and **RETURN** pseudo-instructions are translated to machine instructions to save the return address and return to the calling point.

IntyBASIC is a good compiler but it cannot be as "smart" as a human being as he/she can optimize the machine code down to the last cycle using assembler language.

This is a good example of why it's important to consider using assembler code in critical routines that should be fast.

You can learn more about assembler looking at the example files included with jzintv and in its docs/programming folder. You'll find more details regarding the instruction set in the cp1600_ref.pdf file.

# Appendix A

## IntyBASIC Reference Manual

The latest IntyBASIC reference manual is always included with the latest release of the IntyBASIC compiler. So this reference can get old as the IntyBASIC compiler is updated. This book was written based on version 1.2.9

IntyBASIC is an integer BASIC compiler for Intellivision. It works as a cross-compiler over a PC, Mac or Linux and generates assembler code that can be processed by as1600 (included with the jzintv emulator).

Platforms requirements:

- PC with Windows XP or better.
- Mac OS X 10.6 or better. (universal 32/64-bits binary)
- Linux.

The current limitations are:

- Division and remainder (modulo) operators treat numbers as unsigned.
- The constants 32768-65535 don't imply unsigned numbers, so if these are used in a comparison with a variable, the variable should be marked as UNSIGNED.
- ASM cannot be used inside DEF FN.
- Using PRINT for numbers always show numbers as unsigned from 0 to 65535.

Usage:

```
intybasic in.bas output.asm [library_path]
intybasic --jlp in.bas output.asm [library_path]
intybasic --cc3 in.bas output.asm [library_path]
intybasic --title "My cute game" in.bas output.asm [library_path]
```

The following modules are automatically included as prologue and epilogue of your generated code and they set important variables and helper code:

```
intybasic_prologue.asm
intybasic_epilogue.asm
```

By default these are taken from the current directory unless you choose a library path.

Afterwards you should assemble your program using as1600:

```
as1600 -o output.bin -l output.lst output.asm
```

And finally you can test it using jzintv or Nostalgia emulators:

```
jzintv output.bin        Normal run
jzintv --jlp output.bin  Run with JLP support
jzintv -v1 output.bin    Run with Intellivoice support
```

Alternatively you can load the program into a CuttleCart, Intellicart or LTO-Flash for testing on a real Intellivision.

See below for information about source-level debugging.

The following sample programs are included:

| | |
|---|---|
| samples/bats.bas | Animated bats using new statements for loops |
| samples/constants.bas | Constants library (used by all samples) |
| samples/controller.bas | Test program for controllers |
| samples/envelope.bas | How to use the envelope volume generator of the sound chip |
| samples/flash.bas | Sample of how to use the Flash memory in JLP cartridges. |
| samples/frame.bas | Sample of ON FRAME GOSUB |
| samples/game1.bas | A simple letter-shooting game. |
| samples/game2.bas | A simple labyrinth game with enemies. |
| samples/lander.bas | Lunar Lander-style game |
| samples/music.bas | Simple example of music playing |
| samples/pak.bas | Labyrinth game eating points with ghosts |
| samples/screen.bas | MODE statement test |
| samples/scroll.bas | Example of how to use scrolling. |
| samples/sprites.bas | Moving sprites sample. |
| samples/test.bas | Compiler tester, |
| samples/title.bas | Animated tile for title screen |
| samples/voice.bas | Simple example of Intellivoice |
| | |
| contrib/42k.bas | Example of how to use the 42K words maximum memory map |
| contrib/accel.bas | Moving sprites with subpixel fractions (intvnut) |
| contrib/AppleCatcher.bas | Apple Catcher game by Kiwi |
| contrib/clowns.bas | Clowns & Ballons game by catsfolly |
| contrib/ColouredSquares.bas | Uses Coloured Squares mode to draw Bresenham lines |
| contrib/constants.bas | Constants library (same as samples) |
| contrib/Gram2GromFont.bas | Converts GROM font to different fonts. (by GroovyBee) |
| contrib/hello.bas | Hello World by DZ-Jay |
| contrib/intro.bas | Intro to IntyBASIC by Tarzilla |
| contrib/keypad.bas | Keypad test by GroovyBee |
| contrib/tcg.bas | Trollish Comment Generator by catsfolly |
| contrib/TinyFont.bas | Small font generator at 40 columns (by GroovyBee) |

The following utilities are included:

```
IntyColor    Converts a bitmap image to IntyBASIC source
             code/graphics.
IntySmap     Generates a source-map file to reference
             IntyBASIC source code. Useful with
             the jzintv debugger (option -d and --src-map)
             See section below for full information.
```

# A.1 IntyBASIC language specification

Execution starts at init point of BASIC program.

Syntax per line:

```
[label:] statement[:statement] [' comment][\]

MAIN:    PRINT "HELLO"  ' Prints hello
```

Multiple statements are allowed, but these must be separated by colons.

Variables are created simply by being used.

Labels are created simply by being used.

A variable name starts with a letter or # and is followed by letters, numbers, or the underscore character.

Variables and arrays (see **DIM** and A.5 section for "exact" variables allowed) can be 8-bit (maximum 179 available) or 16-bit in size (maximum 28 available). Variables are 8-bit by default. To define a 16-bit variable use # as the starting character of the variable's name.

```
x
y
#score
```

Notice that if you use the # prefix you should use it everywhere in your program. Variables with the same name but without the # prefix are treated as different 8-bit variables.

All variables are initialized with the value 0 (zero) when they are created. Also, IntyBASIC will warn you if you exceed the number of available variables.

Concatenation of lines is available via the \ character. It concatenates the current line with the following line as a single long line. The following example is completely valid:

```
PR\
    INT\
     "HELL\
    O"
```

And will be processed as PRINT "HELLO"

The following statements are available:

## REM comment

### ' comment

Everything between REM and the end of the line is treated by the compiler as a comment.

## SIGNED name[,name]

Indicates that names are signed variables/arrays.

This only applies to the 8-bit variables that are unsigned by default.

Notice that this adds two machine instructions to extend the sign of each 8-bit signed variable read, although IntyBASIC will try to optimize them.

Usually you can develop your programs without using this keyword, but it's available if you really need it.

## UNSIGNED name[,name]

Indicates that the names are unsigned variables/arrays.

This only applies to the 16-bit variables when doing comparisons of less or greater than, including FOR statements.

Notice that this can add one extra machine instruction to each comparison, this depends on the comparison direction.

This is very useful for score routines up to 65535 or to create subroutines with 32-bit values.

## CONST [name]=[constant expression]

Assigns a name to a constant expression. The compiler will replace all instances of this name, in all expressions, with the number. These names have priority over variable names.

This is like a compiler directive, it doesn't generate code and it can appear anywhere in the program but it will be treated as a constant from the point of appearance onwards.

## GOTO label

Go to label

## GOSUB label

Go to subroutine at label (must be a PROCEDURE).

## label: PROCEDURE

## [code for subroutine]

## END

Creates a PROCEDURE callable by GOSUB.

It's important that PROCEDURE is on the same line as the label.

END implies an automatic RETURN.

**RETURN**

Return from subroutine (PROCEDURE). Also can be used to return early from a PROCEDURE.

**FOR A=start TO end [STEP increment]**

**NEXT**       **' Also supported NEXT A**

**FOR A=1 TO 5 ' Loop**

   **[Variable A will contain 1,2,3,4,5]**

**NEXT A**

**FOR A=1 TO 5 STEP 2**

   **[Variable A will contain 1, 3, 5]**

**NEXT A**

**FOR A=5 TO 1 STEP -2**

   **[Variable A will contain 5, 3, 1]**

**NEXT A**

Looping statement.

The *start, end* and *step* expressions can be complex, instead of only constants or variables.

Notice that you can only use regular variables for the loop variable, not array variables. There is a small quirk if you're using an 8-bit variable and the TO expression is pretty complex and reaches 0 or 255, the loop can be infinite.

## WHILE expr:[statement]:WEND

## WHILE expr

### [statement]

## WEND

Looping statement that keeps looping as long as the expression evaluates to non-zero.

## DO WHILE expr:[statement]:LOOP

## DO WHILE expr

### [statement]

## LOOP


## DO UNTIL expr:[statement]:LOOP

## DO UNTIL expr

### [statement]

## LOOP

**DO:[statement]:LOOP WHILE expr**

**DO**

    **[statement]**

**LOOP WHILE expr**


**DO:[statement]:LOOP UNTIL expr**

**DO**

    **[statement]**

**LOOP UNTIL expr**

Looping statements that keep looping WHILE expression evaluates to non-zero, or UNTIL expression evaluates to non-zero.

**EXIT FOR**

Exits current FOR loop, jumps directly to the line that follows NEXT.

**EXIT WHILE**

Exits current WHILE loop, jumps directly to the line that follows WEND.

**EXIT DO**

Exits current DO loop, jumps directly to the line that follows LOOP.

**IF expr GOTO [label]**

**IF expr THEN [statement]**

**IF expr THEN [statement] ELSE [statement]**


**IF expr THEN**

  **[statement]**

**END IF**


**IF expr THEN**

  **[statement]**

**ELSE**

  **[statement]**

**END IF**


**IF expr THEN**

  **[statement]**

**ELSEIF expr THEN**

  **[statement]**

**END IF**

**IF expr THEN**

  **[statement]**

**ELSEIF expr THEN**

  **[statement]**

**ELSE**

  **[statement]**

**END IF**

Decision statement

**ON expr GOTO [label],[label],[label]**

**ON expr GOTO [label],,[label]**

**ON expr GOTO ,,[label]**

**ON expr GOSUB [label],[label],[label]**

**ON expr GOSUB [label],,[label]**

**ON expr GOSUB ,,[label]**

Decision statement

The expression is evaluated and if the result is zero, the first label is taken, if the result is one, the second label is taken, and successively up to any number of labels.

If GOSUB is used then you must make sure that each label is linked to a PROCEDURE.

If an option has no label or if the expression exceeds the number of labels, the execution flow continues with the following statement after ON.

## ON FRAME GOSUB label

On each video frame interrupt, the IntyBASIC core will call the indicated PROCEDURE.

This doesn't generate any code and should only appear once in your program. Also, it's important to keep in mind this procedure could be called even before your initialization routines are executed.

The only valid assumption is that every single variable is zero after booting.

Also it's your responsability that the code doesn't take too long to execute, otherwise video frame interrupts will accumulate and your memory stack will overflow.

## POKE address,data

Poke memory with data

## WAIT

Waits for the next frame interruption (1/60 of a second for NTSC or 1/50 of a second for PAL)

## OPTION WARNINGS ON

## OPTION WARNINGS OFF

Enable/disable the compilation warnings. Notice that if you disable warnings at the end of your program, you will not have the list of non-used variables.

## OPTION EXPLICIT

## OPTION EXPLICIT ON

## OPTION EXPLICIT OFF

Makes it mandatory to declare each variable with DIM before said variable can be used.

## DIM variable

## DIM variable[,variable]

Declares a variable.

Useful in combination with OPTION EXPLICIT.

UNSIGNED and SIGNED are still applied separately.

## DIM var(size)

Creates an array of data called 'var' of size 'size' elements. Counting starts at zero, so DIM A(10) creates an array of 0 to 9.

You can also create arrays of 16-bit numbers, using DIM #B(10)

The array can be accessed as follows:

A(1)=A(1)+5

A(X)=A(Y)-2

The DIM statement is like a directive, meaning it doesn't generate code and it can appear anywhere in the program. The definition will start from the line of the DIM statement.

## RESTORE label

## READ var

## READ var,var2

## label:

### DATA constant_expr[,constant_expr]

### DATA string

**DATA PACKED string**

**DATA PACKED constant_expr[,constant_expr]**

**DATA VARPTR a**

**DATA VARPTR b(constant_expr)**

The RESTORE statement will reset an internal pointer to the indicated label that should be annex to a DATA statement, this is useful for defining tables and/or graphics.

Numbers can be in the 16-bit range. READ will automatically limit to variable size, for example if 16-bit data is read into a 8-bit variable, it will translate only the lower 8-bit.

READ A          ' Reads data into A, limiting to 8 bits

READ #A         ' Reads data into #A, no limitations.

                ' Notice A and #A are different variables.

READ A(B)       ' Reads data into A(B)

READ #A(B)      ' Reads data into #A(B)

After reading a value, the internal pointer will point to the following value.

All data contained in DATA can also be accessed using the familiar array-indexing syntax, like this:

FOR A=0 TO 4

PRINT AT TABLE(A),"Z"

NEXT A


TABLE:

DATA 21,42,63,84,105


String data will be converted to Intellivision character codes (just like with PRINT but not multiplied by 8 for the screen)

The string data with DATA PACKED will store two Intellivision character codes per word (higher byte of word contains first letter, lower byte of word contains following letter).

The constant data with DATA PACKED will be handled the same way. If DATA PACKED is given an odd number of bytes to process, it will add a zero byte to complete the last word.

**DEFINE card_num,total,label**

**DEFINE card_num,total,VARPTR label(expr)**

**DEFINE ALTERNATE card_num,total,label**

**DEFINE ALTERNATE card_num,total,VARPTR label(expr)**

Loads graphics into GRAM "card_num" (0-63) for a total of "total" cards. label points to the graphics (DATA or BITMAP).

Label can also reference a 16-bit array for dynamically defined GRAM (different from the static ones preserved in Read-Only Memory or ROM)

DIM #graphic(4)

DEFINE 0,1,#graphic

And the VARPTR syntax allows us to select a bitmap from multiple definitions.

The graphics will be loaded in the next video frame (you can use a WAIT to synchronize with the loading).

Notice that there is an approximate limit of 18 GRAM cards that can be loaded per frame (this was measured with an emulator in NTSC mode).

This limit is reduced to 16 GRAM cards per frame when using the music player (when using the PLAY statement).

Notice that there are two variants, namely DEFINE and DEFINE ALTERNATE. This allows you to change two cards sets in one frame. This can be useful because if you use DEFINE multiple times per frame only the latest one is taken in account.

**SOUND 0,[VALUE 12 bits],[VOL 0-15]  Channel A**

**SOUND 1,[VALUE 12 bits],[VOL 0-15]  Channel B**

**SOUND 2,[VALUE 12 bits],[VOL 0-15]  Channel C**

**SOUND 3,[VALUE 16 bits],[TYPE 0-15] Volume envelope (frequency/shape)**

**SOUND 4,[NOISE 5 bits],[MIX] Noise and mix register ($38 value by default)**

The following SOUND 5 to 9 is only usable with the secondary PSG in the ECS add-on module

**SOUND 5,[VALUE 12 bits],[VOL 0-15]  Channel A**

**SOUND 6,[VALUE 12 bits],[VOL 0-15]  Channel B**

**SOUND 7,[VALUE 12 bits],[VOL 0-15]  Channel C**

**SOUND 8,[VALUE 16 bits],[TYPE 0-15] Volume envelope (frequency/shape)**

**SOUND 9,[NOISE 5 bits],[MIX] Noise and mix register ($38 value by default)**

The desired frequency value can be calculated as:

value = (3579545 / 32 / frec)

Please take note of this change for PAL consoles:

value = (4000000 / 32 / frec)

Only a constant (0 to 9) can be used as the first parameter of SOUND.

For channels A, B and C, if you use volume 48 then PSG will use the volume envelope (see SOUND 3 and Appendix B)

Use volume 0 to deactivate tone channels instead of the mixer bits. Also don't use a zero value for the frequency parameter in channel A, B or C, it's better to use 1 in order to get a fast response when changing frequency.

More info about the PSG at:

```
http://spatula-city.org/~im14u2c/intv/jzintv-1.0-beta3/doc/
programming/psg.txt
http://spatula-city.org/~im14u2c/intv/
gi_micro_programmable_tv_games/page_7_100.png
http://spatula-city.org/~im14u2c/intv/
gi_micro_programmable_tv_games/page_7_101.png
http://spatula-city.org/~im14u2c/intv/
gi_micro_programmable_tv_games/page_7_102.png
http://spatula-city.org/~im14u2c/intv/
gi_micro_programmable_tv_games/page_7_103.png
http://spatula-city.org/~im14u2c/intv/
gi_micro_programmable_tv_games/page_7_104.png
http://spatula-city.org/~im14u2c/intv/
gi_micro_programmable_tv_games/page_7_105.png
```

If you use the music player, the SOUND capabilities are affected. Refer to the PLAY statement later in this appendix for further information.

### SPRITE index,x,y,f

The first parameter indicates the number of the MOB (0 to 7). Notice that if you use a constant the generated code will be faster. Sprites (MOBs) will be updated during the next frame.

X contains coordinate X (0 to 168)

bit 8 = Interaction (suggested always 1)

bit 9 = Visibility (suggested always 1)

bit 10 = Double size X

Y contains coordinate Y (0 to 104)

bit 7 = Draw 16-line sprite (it should be aligned in even GRAM boundary 0/2/4/8 etc.)

bits 9-8 = Scale 00= 0.5x, 01= 1x, 10= 2x, 11= 4x

bit 10 = X flip

bit 11 = Y flip


F contains color and card number

bits 2-0 = Lower bits of color

bits 11-3 = Card number (0-255 for GROM, 256-319 for GRAM)

bit 12 = Upper bit of color

bit 13 = Change color stack.

The X,Y,F values are written as-is to the STIC. Please check the specifications at:

http://spatula-city.org/~im14u2c/intv/jzintv-1.0-beta3/doc/programming/stic.txt

## CLS

Clears the screen. All card are set to 0.

Also resets the internal cursor position to the top-left corner of the screen.

## PRINT [AT [expr]][COLOR [expr]][,]"string"[,"string"]

Prints the given string at the current cursor coordinate (or selected via the AT value 0 to 239).

The string is automatically converted from ASCII to Intellivision characters and XORed with the current color ($0000-$0007, $1000-$1007 or $2000 for color stack)

For Foreground/Background mode, use $0000-$0007, and $0200 is bit 0 of the background color, $0400 is bit 1 of the background color,

$1000 is bit 2 of the background color and $2000 is bit 3 of the background color. See the MODE statement below for more information.

Notice that the cursor position is not limited so you can write outside of the screen and this will make your program crash!

If you want to use a character in GROM beyond character 95 or GRAM characters 256 to 319 you can use the inverted slash as an escape character (by example "\96\256\319").

If you want to use double quotes inside a string you can escape it this way: \"

Examples of positioning:

```
PRINT AT 0,"A"       ' for upper-left corner
PRINT AT 19,"B"      ' for upper-right corner
PRINT AT 220,"C"     ' for bottom-left corner
PRINT AT 239,"D"     ' for bottom-right corner
```

Example:

```
PRINT AT 84 COLOR (RAND AND 7),"HELLO WORLD"
PRINT "HELLO WORLD" ' Starts at previous cursor position

PRINT <>expr' Simple number
PRINT <const>expr    ' Left-padded with zeroes to 'const' size.
PRINT <.const>expr    ' Left-paded with spaces to 'const' size.
```

Prints a decimal number at the current position using the current color. You can add the AT and COLOR options.

Example:

PRINT AT 5 COLOR 6,"Score:",<6>#score,"00"

## PRINT [AT [expr],]expr[,expr]

Pokes a 12-bits value directly into the screen, which is useful for variable things and GRAM cards.

For format information please check the STIC specification cited upwards or the F parameter of the SPRITE statement.

This also increases the cursor position.

Example: Printing a digit in yellow:

PRINT (DIGIT+16)*8+6

## SCROLL [offset_x],[offset_y],[move_screen]

Allows you to scroll the screen pixel by pixel. Offset X and Y can be any number between 0 and 7.

Once you pass the frontier of 8 pixels, you can specify how to move all cards on the screen with the move_screen parameter:

1 = Scroll leftwards

2 = Scroll rightwards

3 = Scroll upwards

4 = Scroll downwards

The command will be processed during the next frame or interrupt.

Notice that if you use the SCROLL statement anywhere in your program, the number of available 16-bit variables will be decreased automatically, because IntyBASIC uses some 16-bit variables for buffering purposes, and it will generate extra code for scrolling.

Also notice that the Intellivision video chip (STIC) requires you to correct the position of every sprite when using scrolling. See the sample program SCROLL.BAS for an example.

## BORDER [color],[mask]

Allows you to choose the border color, and also to mask the edges for scrolling.

color can be any number between 0 and 15.

mask can be 0, 1 (mask left column), 2 (mask top row) or 3 (mask both left and top rows)

Border and mask will be updated in the next frame.

## MODE 0,color1,color2,color3,color4

## MODE 1

Sets the video mode (Color Stack mode or Foreground/Background mode). This happens in the next video frame (you can synchronize with the WAIT statement)

Notice that you cannot use PRINT COLOR until the next WAIT statement has been executed, because the color variable is used to save data. After this COLOR will be reset to 7.

In Color Stack mode you can choose the four background colors available in the range 0 to 15.

In Foreground/Background mode you have access to 16 background colors but you can only use cards 0 to 63 (basic character set and uppercase letters) and the defined cards 256 to 319.

By default IntyBASIC starts in Color Stack mode.

## SCREEN label[,origin_offset,target_offset,cols,rows]

## SCREEN
label[,origin_offset,target_offset,cols,rows,origin_width]

This statement is the fastest way to copy screen data to video. Using only "SCREEN label" copies a full screen of 20x12 cards to video.

'label' points to a label inside your program containing the data for the screen, similar to this:

my_screen:

DATA $0007,$000F,$0007,$000F  ' And so…

origin_offset is the offset (0 to 199 or bigger) inside the origin screen

target_offset is the offset (0 to 199) inside the target video screen.

cols is the horizontal size (number of columns) of your copy.

rows is the vertical size (number of rows) of your copy.

origin_width is the origin screen width, useful to copy a sub-portion of a big graphic screen, like a map or when scrolling horizontally. If this parameter is not used, the default value is 20, which corresponds to the Intellivision screen width.

This can serve to move large elements in video, or to display beautiful graphic screens.

Label can be also a 16-bit array for dynamically-drawn elements.

```
DIM #cards(4)
SCREEN #cards,0,0,4,1
```

## BITMAP "00000000"

## BITMAP "00001111"

## BITMAP "_____"

## BITMAP "___XXXX"

Allows you to draw using binary data. You should put BITMAP statements in pairs as they are declared in assembler using DECLE.

This is most useful when attaching a label and using with DEFINE.

Characters interpreted as zero include: "0" "_" " " "."

All other characters will be interpreted as one.

## PLAY SIMPLE

## PLAY SIMPLE NO DRUMS

## PLAY FULL

## PLAY FULL NO DRUMS

Activates the music player and selects the type of music to be played. SIMPLE only uses two channels, allowing the programmer to use SOUND 2 for sound effects.

FULL uses all three channels, so SOUND cannot be used in this context.

The music player plays drums using the noise channel and the mix register. You can deactivate this feature using the NO DRUMS syntax, for example if you want to generate explosion sounds with the noise channel, allowing you to use SOUND 4.

Notice that the music player will update the sound channels on every video frame.

Also notice that if you use the NO DRUMS syntax, you must insert the following statement just after the PLAY statement in order to set the mix register correctly (the player will not modify it):

```
SOUND 4,,$38
```

## PLAY NONE

Deactivates the music player. Following this the programmer should turn off all the sound channels, using this code:

```
SOUND 0,1,0
SOUND 1,1,0
SOUND 2,1,0
SOUND 4,1,$38
```

## PLAY VOLUME expr

Sets the volume for music playing. 0 is silence, 1 is minimum volume, 15 is maximum volume.

If you use this statement, don't forget to put PLAY VOLUME 15 at the start of your program, because volume will be 0 at start (silence).

Notice that this will cause the inclusion of extra code inside your program (around 300 words) and will use a few more cycles during each video frame.

## PLAY label

Plays the music pointed by 'label'.

label can also be a 16-bit array for loading dynamically-generated music.

IntyBASIC will automatically include extra code for the music player.

Music must be in this format: (each MUSIC statement can contain up to 8 arguments)

```
label:    DATA 8  ' Ticks per note (50 ticks per second)
          MUSIC F4,A4#,C5
          MUSIC S,S,S
          MUSIC -,-,-


MUSIC REPEAT
MUSIC STOP
MUSIC JUMP label      ' Jump to label (useful for separating intro
                      ' in looping music)


MUSIC C4,F4,-         ' Notice how C4 extends along 4 tempos
                      ' and F4 only 2
```

MUSIC S,S,-

MUSIC S,-,-

MUSIC S,-,-

Identifiers for notes: Note C, D, E, F, G, A, B followed by octave (2-6), C7 is also available.

Optionally add the # symbol for sharp. Optionally add W, X, Y or Z to specify the instrument (W for piano, X for clarinet, Y for flute, Z for bass).

Setting the instrument carries over in each channel for MUSIC statements played afterwards if the instrument is not specified thereafter.

Notice that the instruments waveforms can be altered by modifying the *intybasic_epilogue.asm* file for your program.

Also the programmer can put S to sustain the previous note, or he can put - for silence.

The fourth/eight argument for MUSIC allows for simple drums. Valid values are: - for none, M1 for strong, M2 for tap, M3 for roll.

IntyBASIC will automatically detect PAL/NTSC Intellivision and will adjust the music's timing and frequencies accordingly.

## PLAY OFF

Stops the music, if music is currently playing.

## VOICE INIT

Initializes the Intellivoice support. It should be called only one time at start of your program or the Intellivoice could hang the system.

The usage of any VOICE statement will cause IntyBASIC to automatically include extra code for Intellivoice support at the start of the program.

## VOICE PLAY label

Lets the Intellivoice perform the voice speech indicated by label.

If there is another phrase being spoken or queued then it will be placed at the end of the queue.

If the queue is full then the phrase will be lost.

label can be a 16-bit array in order to build phrases dynamically.

### VOICE PLAY WAIT label

Starts a voice speech in the same way as VOICE PLAY but it will continue the execution until all phrases in the queue have been spoken.

label can be an 16-bit array in order to build phrases dynamically.

### VOICE WAIT

Waits for the voice queue to be empty.

### VOICE NUMBER expr

Causes the Intellivoice to say the given expression as a number. It works the same as with VOICE PLAY, meaning it will be placed at the end of the queue if the queue is not empty.

### VOICE phrases[,phrases]

Data for phrases. Use 0 to finish a phrase. For example:

```
        VOICE INIT
        VOICE PLAY WAIT numbers
        VOICE PLAY WAIT lets_play
        VOICE NUMBER 147
loop:
        GOTO loop
numbers:
        VOICE ONE,THREE,SIX,HUNDRED,0
lets_play:
        VOICE LL, EH, EH, PA1, TT2, SS
```

VOICE PA2, PP, LL, EH, EY, PA2, 0

Allowed phrases are:

PA5, PA4, PA3, PA2, PA1

MATTEL, ZERO, ONE, TWO, THREE, FOUR, FIVE,

SIX, SEVEN, EIGHT, NINE, TEN, ELEVEN,

TWELVE, THIRTEEN, FOURTEEN, FIFTEEN, SIXTEEN,

SEVENTEEN, EIGHTEEN, NINETEEN, TWENTY, THIRTY,

FOURTY, FIFTY, SIXTY, SEVENTY

EIGHTY, NINETY, HUNDRED, THOUSAND, TEEN, TY,

PRESS, ENTER, OR, AND

AA, AE1, AO, AR, AW, AX, AY, BB1,

BB2, CH, DD1, DD2, DH1, DH2, EH,

EL, ER1, ER2, EY, FF, GG1, GG2, GG3,

HH1, HH2, IH, IY, JH, KK1,

KK2, KK3, LL, MM, NG1, NN1, NN2, OR2,

OW, OY, PP, RR1, RR2, SH, SS

TH, TT1, TT2, UH, UW1, UW2, VV, WH,

WW, XR2, YR, YY1, YY2, ZH, ZZ

## FLASH INIT

This should be the first thing called if you're using the FLASH functions.

It only needs to appear once at the start of the program code.

The default size is 16, equivalent to 128 rows of Flash memory.

## FLASH ERASE row

Erases the row number specified by the expression. The row number can be any value between FLASH.FIRST to FLASH.LAST.

It erases a *full sector* which is a multiple of 8 rows. So erasing any row in a multiple of 8 will erase the 8 consecutive rows.

Note: You need to invoke IntyBASIC with the --jlp command line option.

### FLASH READ row,VARPTR #array(0)

Reads the row number given by the expression and copies the content inside the given 16-bit array. This array must contain at least 96 values. The row number can range from FLASH.FIRST to FLASH.LAST.

Note: You need to invoke IntyBASIC with the --jlp command line option.

### FLASH WRITE row,VARPTR #array(0)

Writes the contents of an array of 16-bit values (the array must contain at least 96 elements) in the flash memory at the given row number. The row number can range from FLASH.FIRST to FLASH.LAST.

Notice that it can write only to an *erased* row, this means that once a row is written it cannot be written to again until its sector is erased.

Note: You need to invoke IntyBASIC with the --jlp command line option.

Don't forget to use the option --jlp in jzintv and --jlp-savegame=file

WARNING: YOUR INTYBASIC PROGRAM WILL TURN THE SCREEN BLACK AND STOP FOR A FEW MILLISECONDS WHILE THE JLP FLASH OPERATION IS PERFORMED, THIS INCLUDES ANY BACKGROUND MUSIC.

### DEF FN func = RAND % 10

### DEF FN screen_off(row, col) = (row * 20 + col)

### DEF FN resetsprite(number) = SPRITE number,0

Allows the programmer to define functions with any number of arguments.

Notice that these are processed like macros: The arguments are replaced as-is and the text of the function is inserted as-is after argument replacement. (because of that are included the extra parenthesis in the screen_off expression)

For example, the two functions screen_off and resetsprite could be called as:

> A = func
>
> PRINT AT screen_off(4,8),"HELLO!"
>
> resetsprite(0)

Please notice that although it's possible to reuse internal function names, when called the internal functions have priority over DEF FN (DEF FN is ignored)

## STACK_CHECK

This statement, if it appears anywhere in your program, will activate a sub-routine that will continuously check for stack overflow in the video interrupt routine.

If the stack exceeds the allowed limit, the sub-routine will stop the program and show a prominent error message on the screen saying "Stack overflow".

This happens commonly when jumping to a PROCEDURE with GOSUB and getting out of the PROCEDURE with GOTO instead of RETURN.

## INCLUDE "filename.bas"

Includes de contents of another source file inside the current IntyBASIC program. Notice that you cannot use INCLUDE recursively.

Also, INCLUDE allows you to include external code anywhere in your program. You could even have half of a procedure in the main file and the rest of it in the included file.

This is very useful for separating graphics and screen files.

When looking for the file to include, the compiler will first look in the current directory and if the source file is not found there, it will look in the library path provided in the command line.

## CALL NAME

Calls the assembly function NAME without arguments. Note IntyBASIC will put the NAME all in uppercase.

## CALL NAME(expr)

Calls the assembly function NAME with one argument in register R0.

## CALL NAME(expr,expr)

Calls the assembly function NAME with two arguments in registers R0 and R1 (up to 4 are allowed).

## ASM code

Allows you to insert assembly code directly into your source code. The line content is copied directly to output. It's also very useful to include assembly code modules, like this:

```
ASM INCLUDE "yourfile.asm"
```

# A.2 Expression syntax

The expression syntax is like a calculator.

The usual precedence rules apply to expression operators. Addition and substraction have lower precedence than multiplication and division. This means $1 + 2 * 3 = 7$ not 9.

| | |
|---|---|
| A=5 | Decimal number |
| A=$1000 | Hexadecimal number |
| A=&10101 | Binary number |

| | |
|---|---|
| A="C" | Intellivision card code for letter. |
| A=B | Simple assignment |
| A=A+B | Simple addition |
| A=A-B | Simple substraction |
| A=A*B | Simple multiplication |

Multiplication by 2/4/8/16/32/64/128/256/512/1024/2048/4096 is internally optimized.

Multiplication by constants less than 128 is optimized with a macro.

Multiplication uses a shift algorithm that is relatively efficient for most cases. (42 cycles minimum or 702 cycles in worst case)

Multiplication of variable by variable uses intvnut's fast multiply routine (fixed 272 cycles)

When using the --jlp switch the multiplication is accelerated by hardware.

A=A/B        Simple unsigned division (done by repeated substraction, which can be slow)

Division by 2/4/8/16/32/64/128/256 is internally optimized.

Division of variable by variable uses my fast division routine (214 to 517 cycles)

When using the --jlp switch the division is accelerated by hardware

A=A%B        Simple unsigned remainder

Notice that it calculates the remainder by repeated substraction (which can be slow)

Remainder by powers of 2 internally uses AND.

Remainder of variable by variable uses my fast remainder routine (214 to 517 cycles)

A=(A+B)-C

A=A AND B

A=A OR B          Notice that this operation is not native, so it's not efficient.

A=A XOR B

A=NOT A

A=-A

A=A=B             If A and B are the same then the result is $ffff (-1) else zero

A=A<>B

A=A<B

A=A>B

A=A<=B

A=A>=B

A=PEEK(expr) Reads a memory location.

PEEK always reads a value of 16 bits that can be processed in an expression.

A=ABS(expr)   Gets absolute value of expression (non-negative).

A=SGN(expr)   Gets sign of expression (-1, 0 or 1)

A=array(expr)  Accesses an array. The array can be defined with DIM or label for DATA.

array(expr)=A  Writes data to an array. The array can be defined with DIM. DATA is not writable.

A =USR NAME

Calls assembly function **NAME** (all in uppercase) without arguments.

A=USR NAME(expr)

Calls assembly function **NAME** with one argument in register R0.

A=USR NAME(expr,expr)

Calls assembly function **NAME** with two arguments in registers R0 and R1 (up to 4 allowed).

Assembly functions can put results in register R0.

#A=VARPTR B

Gets a pointer to a variable. Useful when linking assembler routines.

#A=VARPTR C(0)

Gets pointer to an array. Can be defined with **DIM** or label for **DATA**.

CONT              Contains AND'ed $01fe and $01ff complemented content (from both controllers).

CONT.UP           Non-zero if the player presses up on the disc of either controller.

CONT.DOWN         Non-zero if the player presses down on the disc of either controller.

CONT.LEFT         Non-zero if the player presses left on the disc of either controller.

CONT.RIGHT        Non-zero if the player presses right on the disc of either controller.

CONT.BUTTON       Non-zero if any button is pressed on either controller.

| | |
|---|---|
| CONT.B0 | Non-zero if either top button is pressed on either controller. |
| CONT.B1 | Non-zero if bottom left button is pressed on either controller. |
| CONT.B2 | Non-zero if bottom right button is pressed on either controller. |
| CONT.KEY | Currently pressed keypad key on either controller (0 to 9 for numbers, 10=Clear, 11=Enter, 12=Not pressed). |

Because disc movements can be processed as keypad inputs, it's suggested to wait for CONT.KEY to contain 12 before waiting for a key.

| | |
|---|---|
| CONT1 | Contains complemented content of address $01ff (left controller) |
| CONT1.UP | Non-zero if the player presses up on the disc of the left controller. |
| CONT1.DOWN | Non-zero if the player presses down on the disc of the left controller. |
| CONT1.LEFT | Non-zero if the player presses left on the disc of the left controller. |
| CONT1.RIGHT | Non-zero if the player presses right on the disc of the left controller. |
| CONT1.BUTTON | Non-zero if any button is pressed on the left controller. |
| CONT1.B0 | Non-zero if either top button is pressed on the left controller. |
| CONT1.B1 | Non-zero if the bottom left button is pressed on the left controller. |
| CONT1.B2 | Non-zero if the bottom right button is pressed on |

the left controller.

CONT1.KEY    Currently pressed keypad key on the left controller
             (0 to 9 for numbers, 10=Clear, 11=Enter,
             12=Not pressed)

Because disc movements can be processed as keypad inputs, it's suggested to wait for CONT1.KEY to contain 12 before waiting for a key.

CONT2          Contains complemented content of address $01fe
               (right controller)

CONT2.UP       Non-zero if the player presses up on the disc of
               the right controller.

CONT2.DOWN Non-zero if the player presses down on the disc of
               the right controller.

CONT2.LEFT    Non-zero if the player presses left on the disc of
               the right controller.

CONT2.RIGHT Non-zero if the player presses right on the disc of
               the right controller.

CONT2.BUTTON       Non-zero if any button is pressed on the
               right controller.

CONT2.B0       Non-zero if either top button is pressed on the
               right controller.

CONT2.B1       Non-zero if the bottom left button pressed on the
               right controller.

CONT2.B2       Non-zero if the bottom right button pressed on the
               right controller.

CONT2.KEY     Currently pressed keypad key on the right
               controller (0 to 9 for numbers, 10=Clear,
               11=Enter, 12=Not pressed)

Because disc movements can be processed as keypad inputs, it's suggested to wait for CONT2.KEY to contain 12 before waiting for a key.

Notice that using the .KEY syntax will produce extra machine code inside IntyBASIC, and you should use WAIT before reading .KEY again, because IntyBASIC processes controller input and decodes keys during each video frame. Remember this uses extra processor time.

Here is some useful code to avoid having key presses processed as disc movements:

```
c = cont2.button
IF (c = $20)+(c = $40)+(c = $80) THEN GOTO skip_disc   ' Ignore keys
    ...disc testing...
skip_disc:
```

| | |
|---|---|
| CONT3 | Contains complemented content of address $00ff (ECS left controller) |
| CONT3.UP | Non-zero if the player presses up on the disc of the ECS left controller. |
| CONT3.DOWN | Non-zero if the player presses down on the disc of the ECS left controller. |
| CONT3.LEFT | Non-zero if the player presses left on the disc of the ECS left controller. |
| CONT3.RIGHT | Non-zero if the player presses right on the disc of the ECS left controller. |
| CONT3.BUTTON | Non-zero if any button is pressed on the ECS left controller. |
| CONT3.B0 | Non-zero if either top button is pressed on the ECS left controller. |
| CONT3.B1 | Non-zero if the bottom left button is pressed on the ECS left controller. |
| CONT3.B2 | Non-zero if the bottom right button is pressed on |

the ECS left controller.

CONT4    Contains complemented content of address $00fe
         (ECS right controller)

CONT4.UP    Non-zero if the player presses up on the disc of
            the ECS right controller.

CONT4.DOWN Non-zero if the player presses down on the disc of
           the ECS right controller.

CONT4.LEFT  Non-zero if the player presses left on the disc of
            the ECS right controller.

CONT4.RIGHT Non-zero if the player presses right on the disc of
            the ECS right controller.

CONT4.BUTTON      Non-zero if any button is pressed on the
                  ECS right controller.

CONT4.B0    Non-zero if either top button is pressed on the
            ECS right controller.

CONT4.B1    Non-zero if the bottom left button is pressed on
            the ECS right controller.

CONT4.B2    Non-zero if the bottom right button is pressed on
            the ECS right controller.

COL0

COL1

COL2

COL3

COL4

COL5

COL6

COL7

         Returns the collision status between sprites for the current frame. It is best to use these after WAIT.

Don't forget to set the interaction bit in sprites (bit 8 of X-coordinate).

bit 0-7 means collision against sprite number.

bit 8 means collision against background pixel (pixel set).

bit 9 means collision against borders.

RAND

Produces a pseudo-random value between 0 and 255.

The value produced is different on each video frame.

RAND(range)

Produces a pseudo-random value between 0 and range-1.

The value produced is different on each video frame.

Notice that it's slower to generate, and the value will be generated faster if based on powers of 2. The maximum range value is 256.

RANDOM(range)

Produces a pseudo-random value between 0 and range-1.

This forces the update of the random number (it doesn't need a WAIT to change). Notice that it's slower to generate, and the value will be generated faster if based on powers of 2. The maximum range value is 256.

LEN(string)

Returns the length of a string. Very useful in combination with DEF FN, for example, for creating strings centered on the screen.

POS(expr)

Returns the current screen position (useful for PRINT AT). The expression is analyzed but no code is generated.

**FRAME**

> Returns the current frame number (0-65535, it cycles back to 0 after reaching 65535)

**NTSC**

> Returns 1 if the Intellivision is an NTSC console, otherwise returns zero.

**#MOBSHADOW(x)**

> Use this to access elements in the MOB buffer (the place where the SPRITE data is saved).
>
> The indexes 0 to 23 correspond exactly to the locations 0 to 23 of the STIC.

**#BACKTAB(x)**

> Use this to access elements in the screen buffer (located at $0200-$02EF)

**FLASH.FIRST**

> Returns the first readable/writable row of JLP Flash memory

**FLASH.LAST**

> Returns the last readable/writable row of JLP Flash memory

**MUSIC.PLAYING**

> Returns zero if music is not currently playing, returns a non-zero value otherwise.

**VOICE.AVAILABLE**

> Returns a non-zero value if the Intellivoice module is detected, otherwise returns zero.

**VOICE.PLAYING**

> Returns a non-zero value if the Intellivoice is currently

playing samples, otherwise returns zero.

# A.3 Assembly language interfacing

The USR expression and the CALL statement allow you to call assembly language modules from inside IntyBASIC programs. Note the label name for assembly language modules is translated to uppercase.

IntyBASIC expect the following conventions to be preserved:


Before calling:

R0 = Value of first argument (or trash)

R1 = Value of second argument (or trash)

R2 = Value of third argument (or trash)

R3 = Value of fourth argument (or trash)

R4 = Trash

R5 = Location to return


After calling:

R0 = Value from assembly language module (only USR expr.)

R1 = Not important

R2 = Not important

R3 = Not important

R4 = Not important

R5 = Not important


If your module changes the address of the Stack Pointer (R6) or messes with previous values stored then there is a high probability that the IntyBASIC program will crash.

If your function is relatively simple:

```
ASM MYFUNCTION:   PROC
ASM            ; ... your code...
ASM            JR R5
ASM            ENDP
```

If your function needs more registers or calls nested functions:

```
ASM MYFUNCTION:   PROC
ASM            BEGIN  ; Really it's PSHR R5
ASM            ; ... your code...
ASM            RETURN ; Really it's PULR R7
ASM            ENDP
```

# A.4 Some further notes

A program's execution is sequential unless interrupted by GOTO or GOSUB. In any of your programs you should put GOTO at the end of the main block, otherwise execution could run in undesirable ways. For example:

Example 1:

```
        A = 5
stop:   GOTO stop      ' Prevents BASIC running out of ROM
```

Example 2:

```
        A = 5
stop:   GOTO stop      ' Prevents execution running inside proc.
```

```
test:     PROCEDURE
          END
```

If you insert PROCEDURE, DATA, MUSIC or VOICE data in the middle of the execution sequence, the Intellivision processor will do strange things. So you must put your data at the end of the program or where the execution doesn't reach it.


Example 3:

```
          A = 6
          DATA 5,6,7     ' Bad, this gets executed!
                         ' move it after the GOTO
stop:     GOTO stop
```

The display starts in color-stack mode, and each card of the 20x12 screen can have bit 13 set to 1 so it avances the current pointer to color-stack and changes the background color.

In order to change the 4 color-stack predefined values, you should use this:

```
          MODE 0,1,2,3,4     ' Select blue color as initial color and
                             ' load other 3 colors
```

The color values are in the range 0-15. In order to select foreground/background mode, you should use this:

```
          MODE 1
```

By default, IntyBASIC starts the program at $5000 area. The available space goes up to $6FFF, for a cartridge binary of 16K.

You can measure your program by checking the generated LST file created by the assembler or the CFG file.

In any case, you can insert ASM statements to create bigger programs, like this:

ASM ORG $D000


ASM ORG $F000


This way you can use the areas $D000-$DFFF and $F000-$FFFF. It's easier to manage and calculate available space if you only put data in these areas.

Another way is to look into the generated .lst file. You can see what memory locations are used in the code generated by IntyBASIC.

Using modern Flash cart and homebrew cartridge PCBs allows following addresses to be used without additional programming:

$2000-$2FFF
$5000-$6FFF
$A000-$BFFF
$C100-$FFFF


As a technical note, the use of any ECS feature inside your IntyBASIC program (such as SOUND 5-9, CONT3 or CONT4) will cause your program to boot from $4800 to disable the ECS ROM. This has the extra advantage of disabling the standard Mattel screen that can be seen for a fraction of a second before your software actually starts.

## A.5 Real number of variables allowed

The number of 8-bit variables allowed are:

228

Substract 3 if you use SCROLL

Substract 3 if you use VOICE

Substract 6 if you use the keypad

Substract 26 if you use PLAY

The number of 16-bits variables allowed are:

47 (7962 if using the --jlp or --cc3 switch)

Substract 20 if you use SCROLL or 30 if you also use VOICE

Notice that each byte or word inside an array allocated with DIM counts as one variable.

## A.6 Generating ROM for Nostalgia emulator

By default the as1600 assembler generates a .bin/.cfg pair of files, and both can be copied in the *roms* directory of the Nostalgia emulator for testing your programs.

Alternatively you can convert both files into a single .rom file, using the bin2rom utility included with jzintv:

bin2rom game.bin

It will generate a game.rom file that contains a mix of the .bin and .cfg file and it's easier to test with Nostalgia.

Another alternative is to use the following as1600 invocation to generate the .rom file in one single step:

as1600 -o output -l output.lst output.asm

# A.7 Source code debugging

There is enough information included in the generated ASM file, and with extensive help from intvnut, there is now support for basic debugging with the IntyBASIC source code shown alongside.

You need to compile your program this way:

```
intybasic input.bas output.asm
as1600 -j output.smap -s output.sym -o output.bin -l output.lst
output.asm
intysmap output.smap
jzintv -d output.bin --src-map=output.smap --sym-file=output.sym
```

After this you can use the jzintv debug commands normally.

Notice that under Windows, your main window must be 160 columns or wider. Inside the debugger use the jzintv command >160 to expand the window if necessary.

Also you can add useful metadata in your IntyBASIC code, like title of game, author name, license, date, etc. It will pass through the as1600 assembler, and it will get embedded into the final ROM file..

This information is used by the newest versions of the LTO-Flash software, and it can be read by the rom_metadata utility in the jzintv package.

Some examples of these tags:

```
ASM CFGVAR "name" = "A woman looks for her cat"
ASM CFGVAR "short_name" = "Cat search!"
ASM CFGVAR "author" = "Mindy Cat Lover"
ASM CFGVAR "release_date" = "2018-07-20"
ASM CFGVAR "license" = "public domain"
ASM CFGVAR "music_by" = "Bea U. Ty"
```

The latest reference to these metadata tags is available at http://
spatula-city.org/~im14u2c/intv/jzintv/doc/rom_fmt/id_tag.txt

ç

# Appendix B

## AY-3-8914 reference

The AY-3-8914 sound chip can handle 3 tone channels with independent volume controls, and it also offers an independent noise channel that can be mixed with any of the 3 tone channels or all of them.

Additionally, it includes an envelope volume generator able to generate pretty unique sounds.

IntyBASIC allows you to control all the sound registers using the SOUND statement exclusively, or indirectly through the integrated music tracker using PLAY/MUSIC statements.

For controlling the three tone channels labelled 0 to 2, you use:

```
SOUND 0,period,volume
SOUND 1,period,volume
SOUND 2,period,volume
```

Where 'period' is calculated as:

period = 3579545 / 32 / desired frequency.

For PAL Intellivision, replace 3579545 by 4000000, as the frequency of the sound chip changes.

The volume is a number from 0 to 15 where 0 is silence and 15 is the highest volume. The volume can also be 48, which means it will use the volume from the envelope generator, to control it you use:

```
SOUND 3,value,envelope
```

Where 'value' is calculated as:

$$value = 3579545 / 32 / 16 / desired\_frequency$$

The extra division by 16 is because the envelope is divided in 16 steps dependent on the envelope value.

**Number**      **Envelope shape**

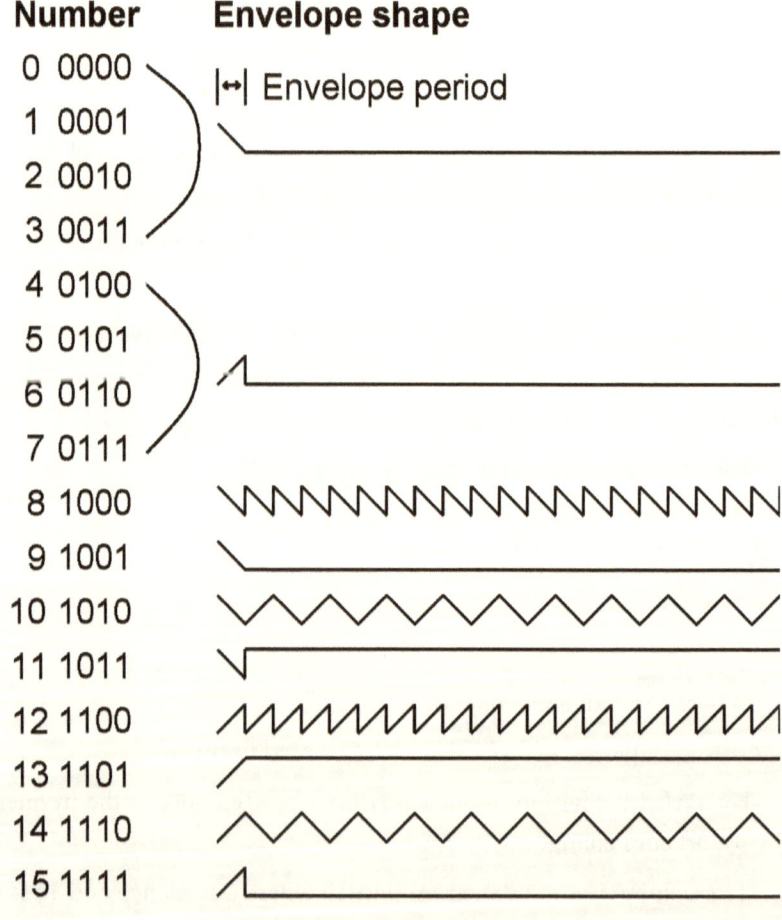

0 0000
1 0001
2 0010
3 0011
4 0100
5 0101
6 0110
7 0111
8 1000
9 1001
10 1010
11 1011
12 1100
13 1101
14 1110
15 1111

To complete this explanation we have:

```
SOUND 4,noise_freq,mixer_bits
```

Where noise_freq is calculated as 3579545 / 256 / noise_freq. The noise generated is a white noise often used for drums and explosions.

The mixer bits are the final step in this trip:

- bit 0 : 0 = Enable tone channel 0, 1 = Disable tone channel 0
- bit 1 : 0 = Enable tone channel 1, 1 = Disable tone channel 1
- bit 2 : 0 = Enable tone channel 2, 1 = Disable tone channel 2
- bit 3 : 0 = Enable noise in ch. 0, 1 = Disable noise in ch. 0
- bit 4 : 0 = Enable noise in ch. 1, 1 = Disable noise in ch. 1
- bit 5 : 0 = Enable noise in ch. 2, 1 = Disable noise in ch. 2
- bit 6 : Should always be 0, or else you will disable hand controllers.
- bit 7 : Should always be 0, or else you will disable hand controllers.

By default, IntyBASIC enables tone and disables noise on all three channels ($38). If you need to mute a channel, you should set that channel's volume to 0, rather than disabling both tone and noise for that channel. Otherwise, you may get an unpleasant popping effect or other distortion. If you're curious why, read on for the details.

The AY-3-8914 mixes tone and noise together on each channel using the following relationship:

channel_out = (tone_signal OR tone_enable) AND (noise_signal OR noise_enable)

Here, tone_signal is the square-wave tone for the channel, and noise_signal is the white noise from the noise generator. This relationship explains why a 1 disables tone/noise, and 0 enables tone/noise. When you enable both tone and noise, the two signals modulate each other, which can make for some interesting sound effects.

When the channel_out is 0, the audio channel outputs no voltage. When channel_out is 1, it outputs a voltage determined by the channel's volume setting. If you disable both tone and noise on a channel, then the channel will output a constant voltage set by that channel's volume setting.

If you set the volume on a channel to a non-zero constant volume (1 to 15) and then disable both tone and noise on that channel, this may result in a "popping" sound. It can also cause sounds on other channels to sound "softer" if you set the volume high enough, due to the way the Intellivision mixes the audio channels. This is why it's usually better to set the volume to 0 to mute a channel.

If you set the volume on a channel to use the envelope instead (48), and then disable both tone and noise on that channel, you can use the envelope generator to make interesting buzzing sound effects.

# Appendix C

## Useful resources

Don't forget to visit the following useful websites for further information about IntyBASIC:

My website pointing to most of these:
http://nanochess.org/intybasic.html

The official IntyBASIC official thread on AtariAge, full of development resources.
http://atariage.com/forums/topic/248209-the-intybasic-compiler-official-thread/

The IntyBASIC 2015 Programming Contest
http://atariage.com/forums/forum/159-intybasic-programming-contest-2015/

The IntyBASIC 2018 Programming Contest
http://atariage.com/forums/forum/194-intybasic-programming-contest-2018/

The AY-3-8910 data sheet
http://map.grauw.nl/resources/sound/generalinstrument_ay-3-8910.pdf

The jzintv emulator, as1600 assembler, CP1610 programming sheet and STIC reference.

http://spatula-city.org/~im14u2c/intv/

The source code for the IntyBASIC compiler.

https://github.com/nanochess/IntyBASIC

My Youtube channel where you can find lots of videos about games developed with IntyBASIC

https://www.youtube.com/channel/UCA5HtS9lDA4nzEbx--3jQpw

# Appendix D

## Source code for rotating smiley

This is the source code in C language for "auto-magically" generating the rotating smiley. It also contains an option to generate it using visual BITMAP statements.

```c
/*
** Generate smiley in 8x16 pixels
**
** by Oscar Toledo G.
**
** Creation date: Nov/23/2017.
*/

#include <stdio.h>
#include <math.h>
#include <stdlib.h>
#include <string.h>

#define PI      3.1415926535897

int my_round(double val)
{
    if (val < 0.0)
        return ceil(val - 0.5);
    return floor(val + 0.5);
}

/*
** Translate coordinate
*/
void translate(int degrees, float x, float y, int *tx, int *ty)
{
```

```
    *tx = my_round((cos(degrees * PI / 180) * x
                    + -sin(degrees * PI / 180) * y) * 2.4) + 4;
    *ty = my_round((sin(degrees * PI / 180) * x
                    + cos(degrees * PI / 180) * y) * 4.8) + 8;
}


/*
** Draw a point
*/
void draw_point(char *bitmap, int x, int y)
{
    if (x < 0 || y < 0 || x > 7 || y > 15) {
        fprintf(stderr, "Exceeded coordinates (%d,%d)\n", x, y);
        return;
    }
    bitmap[y] |= 0x80 >> x;
}


/*
** Draw a line
*/
void draw_line(char *bitmap, int x1, int y1, int x2, int y2)
{
    int x;
    int y;

    x = x1;
    y = y1;
    if (abs(x2 - x1) > abs (y2 - y1)) {
        draw_point(bitmap, x, y);
        while (x != x2) {
            if (x < x2)
                x++;
            else
                x--;
            y = y1 + 1.0 * abs(x - x1) / abs(x2 - x1) * (y2 - y1)
+ 0.5;
            draw_point(bitmap, x, y);
        }
    } else {
        draw_point(bitmap, x, y);
        while (y != y2) {
            if (y < y2)
                y++;
            else
                y--;
            x = x1 + 1.0 * abs(y - y1) / abs(y2 - y1) * (x2 - x1)
+ 0.5;
```

```
                    draw_point(bitmap, x, y);
            }
        }
    }

    /*
    ** Main program
    */
    int main(void)
    {
        int c;
        char bitmap[16];
        int d;
        int x1;
        int y1;
        int x2;
        int y2;
        int x3;
        int y3;
        int x4;
        int y4;
        int x5;
        int y5;
        int x6;
        int y6;

        printf("smiley_bitmaps:\n");
        for (c = 0; c < 360; c += 5) {
            memset(bitmap, 0, sizeof(bitmap));
            translate(c, -1, -1, &x1, &y1);
            translate(c, 1, -1, &x2, &y2);
            translate(c, 1, 1, &x3, &y3);
            translate(c, -1, 1, &x4, &y4);
            translate(c, -0.5, -0.5, &x5, &y5);
            translate(c, 0.5, -0.5, &x6, &y6);
            draw_line(bitmap, x1, y1, x2, y2);
            draw_line(bitmap, x2, y2, x3, y3);
            draw_line(bitmap, x3, y3, x4, y4);
            draw_line(bitmap, x4, y4, x1, y1);
            draw_point(bitmap, x5, y5);
            draw_point(bitmap, x6, y6);
#if 1
            for (d = 0; d < 16; d += 2) {
                if ((d & 7) == 0)
                    printf("\tDATA ");
                printf("$%02x%02x",
                    bitmap[d + 1], bitmap[d]);
                if ((d & 7) == 6) {
```

```c
                        if (d < 8)
                                printf("\t' %d degrees\n", c);
                        else
                                printf("\n");
                } else {
                        printf(",");
                }
        }
#else
        for (d = 0; d < 16; d++) {
                printf("\tBITMAP \"%s%s%s%s%s%s%s%s\"",
                        bitmap[d] & 0x80 ? "X" : ".",
                        bitmap[d] & 0x40 ? "X" : ".",
                        bitmap[d] & 0x20 ? "X" : ".",
                        bitmap[d] & 0x10 ? "X" : ".",
                        bitmap[d] & 0x08 ? "X" : ".",
                        bitmap[d] & 0x04 ? "X" : ".",
                        bitmap[d] & 0x02 ? "X" : ".",
                        bitmap[d] & 0x01 ? "X" : ".");
                if (d == 0)
                        printf("\t' %d degrees", c);
                printf("\n");
        }
#endif
        printf("\n");
    }
    d = 0;
    printf("sin:\n");
    for (c = 0; c < 360; c += 5) {
        x1 = my_round(sin((c - 90) * PI / 180) * 64);
        if ((d & 7) == 0)
                printf("\tDATA ");
        printf("%d", x1);
        if ((d & 7) == 7)
                printf("\n");
        else
                printf(",");
        d++;
    }
}
```

# Appendix E

## About the author

Óscar Toledo Gutiérrez (Mexico, 1978) is an experienced computer programmer.

He has written hundreds of programs in several programming languages, collaborates in the design of the Fenix Operating System and the Biyubi Internet Browser, gives talks at universities and does game design and programming consulting.

He is also the creator of the world's smallest chess programs written in C, Java, Javascript, x86 and 6502 machine code, and also the first Mexican to win the IOCCC (International Obfuscated C Code Contest): Best Game (2005), Best of Show (2007), Best Small Program (2007), Most Portable Chess Set (2007) and Best Non-chess Game (2012), and 2nd place winner at the first JS1K contest (2010).

One of his hobbies is working on classic consoles. He has developed games for MSX, Colecovision, Intellivision, Atari 2600, Sega Master System, Memotech, Spectravideo and Tatung Einstein. His games Princess Quest and Mecha-8 are included in the ColecoVision Flashback retro console by AtGames and he created the IntyBASIC language for programming Intellivision consoles.

He is also the author of the book "Toledo Nanochess: The Commented Source Code" and tweetstar with short stories in Spanish published in @historiasmini and now collected in 3 books.